International acclaim from readers of *The Wealthy Spirit:*

"Chellie is probably going to be the next Suze Orman—she's that good! Her book contains not JUST affirmations, but small daily ACTIONS that move you toward personal and financial success."

—Lin Painchaud-Steinman, Park Edge Books

"I really think your book is brilliant. It was given to me as a gift and I have given it to a number of people myself. What I love about your book is reading short stories EVERY SINGLE DAY. Most books do not reinforce the principles of positive thinking like yours does. I am sure once I hit page 365, I will start all over again. Cheers!"

—Robert S. Grossman, Founder, President & CEO, Focus Creative Group

"I have purchased at least a dozen copies of your book to share with friends! I say your Top 50 Affirmations every morning and every night, and 'people really do love to give me money.' I actually am astounded at how much money has come to me in the last three months....thanks to you! Even my two daughters are open to affirmations and participate with me sometimes. Actually, one morning I had gotten aggravated...my little Sophia (age 9) said, 'Mom, I think it's time for an affirmation'! And, by the way, you said something that I cannot forget and that changed my life. You said to me, 'I love my life.' That one saying has stayed with me. I think of it every day. I love my life!"

—Karen Caplan, President, Frieda's, Inc.

"Have just started reading your absolutely wonderful book. Am not through with it yet despite grabbing every minute I have left from work and chores but am determined to finish reading it soon and start all over again. Your book is very inspiring and I have already sent out ships. Shall keep in touch with you. THANKS A MIL-LION."

—Archana Kulkarni, Mumbai, India

"Thank you so much for all the help your book has given me. I used to get caught up in all the negative things in life, and I never realized that some of the things I used to say and think were actually negative affirmations…I have been reading your book for some time and I am almost done. I can't wait to start reading it again. I am now a full-time realtor living on Cape Cod enjoying my life and making tons of money. I am referred to as "the Realtor with Turn Key Results" now and I owe you a lot of thanks for that. Your book isn't just about money, it's about love and living. I can't believe the turn my life has taken. Thanks for everything."

—Ken Oliver, Realtor

"I just finished Chellie Campbell's book *The Wealthy Spirit*. To you and all those at Sourcebooks whose hands helped bring this book to market, thank you. The book generated so many 'aha!' moments. I read it cover to cover, turning each page with anticipation. Now, I plan to work her book, one day at a time. I've been inspired. Thanks again!"

—Gretchen McKeon, letter to the publisher

"I love your book! In fact, I have used it so much and carry it with me nearly all the time so that it is page-marked, highlighted, 'Post-it-ed,' and dog-eared and looks well, used…During one of my first BIG talks I gave, I used the book to show the audience how sometimes I just open the book, knowing I will get just the message I need. I nearly started crying when the page read: 'No More Fear of Public Speaking.' We all laughed…Thank you. A lot of us were waiting for you to write your book!"

—Fawn Chang, Feng Shui

"I ran a four-week tele-class for therapists recently to help them with their money issues regarding setting, negotiating, and collecting fees from their clients. As a bonus for joining the group, I sent each one a copy of *The Wealthy Spirit*. They have been going crazy over it! They love, love, love it. Just wanted you to know how much you are adored! Blessings to you!"

—Casey Truffo, www.BeAWealthyTherapist.com

"I am currently reading your book *The Wealthy Spirit*. I find your book exceptionally inspirational and confidence building and I thank you for all the work and good will you have put into this book. I live in Sri Lanka. Unfortunately this area was badly affected by the tsunami on the 26th of December 2004. I am doing my daily affirmations as mentioned in your book and I know things will improve…I just want to thank you for giving me that extra push to enable me to get on with my life. Thank you."

—Nilani, email

"I read your book almost every day. Since I started working with the book diligently this summer, my income has tripled! I'm delighted and continue to send out ships as I joyfully receive the riches the other ships are bringing in. Thank you for your amazing work. As a coach I always recommend your book as a textbook for my clients who want to reduce their financial stress. Blessings to you."

—Beth Davis, Life Coach

"I wanted to share a quick story. While I was away, my dad stayed at our house to house sit and watch his 'grand cats.' I had told him about your book and left it for him to read. When I returned he had earmarked so many pages that I know exactly what to give him for Christmas. He can't stop talking about how beneficial all of this is. Go Chellie!"

—Gwendolyn Young, Young Communications Group

"Several months ago, I saw one of my life mentors reading your book. I bought your book and started to read it every day. I find your writing to be serious, funny, down to earth, light to read yet very dense in content. In short, I like your book very much. I keep finding a lot of 'aha!'s from your book…I sincerely thank you for giving me and other people your gift of love, peace, freedom, and inspiration in your writings. I wish you keep soaring with your beautiful work."

—Solihin Jinata, Singapore

"I just had to write to you to tell you that I LOVE your book! The content is great. Your style is warm, friendly, and encouraging. But the format is my favorite part. I love having a quote every day, some content/story, and an affirmation. It totally works for me. I am definitely one of 'your people.' My friends and family are just beside themselves that I'm reading a book for financial stress reduction. They say, 'Exactly what sort of financial stress are you experiencing?' I explain to them that I'm reading it to be a better money manager and for the success of my business. I'm going to start buying copies for everyone I know. Then they'll get it. Thank you for sharing your gifts and talents in the form of this book."

—Carrie Kish, Valencia, California

"I've been reading your affirmations every day. I had written several on a piece of paper to do that day. One of my friends who had cancer was complaining because she had been having chemo and her counts were going up instead of down. I told her not to complain, but instead say an affirmation on her forty-five-minute drive to the doctor. She said to give her one. I looked at my piece of paper and told her to say, 'Something wonderful is happening to me today. I can feel it!' She did what I told her, and she says when she entered the doctor's office the doctor ran out yelling, 'You're cancer-free!' She could not believe it, but she is coming to me for more affirmations. Thanks."

—Y. Garza, Texas

"I'm reading your book and loving it (it's hard to keep to just one page a day)! You've got a fantastic blend of spiritual principles and practical tips…I am definitely one of YOUR people! Thanks for the reminder that the money is in the phone…and thanks for writing such a fabulous book!"

—Donna Cutting, ShowStopping Solutions

"What an incredible book you have written. I wanted to commend you on your work and I hope there is a way the show I produce can spread the word about *The Wealthy Spirit*."
—Michelle Anton, Senior Producer, Dr. Laura Program, Premiere Radio Networks, Inc.

"I just wanted to let you know how much I love your book! The quotes, affirmations, and uplifting stories and philosophy are just terrific. Great job!"
—Lynn Robinson, www.LynnRobinson.com

"Took out this magical book three times at the library. Ordered one at the local bookstore. Before it arrived, my wife had already picked up one for our ten-year anniversary. I'm self-employed. I think she's thinking with the extra income I'll be making from all my ships coming in and affirmations, she'll get a much bigger gift next year. Thanks—this book seems like it was written just for me. Great job! I hope your life is as magical, fun, and blessed as mine."
—Mark, email

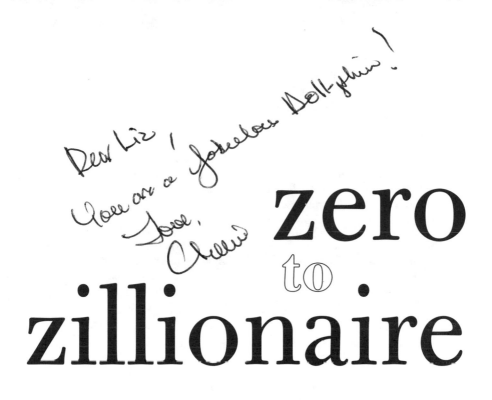

Dear Liz!
You are a fabulous Dolphin!
Love,
Chellie

zero
to
zillionaire

8 Foolproof Steps to Financial Peace of Mind

By Chellie Campbell

SOURCEBOOKS, INC.®
NAPERVILLE, ILLINOIS

Published by Sourcebooks, Inc.
P.O. Box 4410, Naperville, Illinois 60567–4410
(630) 961-3900
Fax: (630) 961-2168
www.sourcebooks.com

Library of Congress Cataloging-in-Publication Data

Campbell, Chellie.
  Zero to zillionaire : 8 foolproof steps to financial peace of mind /
By Chellie Campbell.
    p. cm.
  ISBN-13: 978-1-4022-0619-1
  ISBN-10: 1-4022-0619-4
  1. Money--Psychological aspects. 2. Millionaires--Psychology. 3.
Capitalists and financiers--Psychology. 4. Rich people--Psychology. 5.
Wealth--Psychological aspects. 6. Success in business--Psychological
aspects. I. Title.

HG222.3.C36 2006
332.024'01--dc22

2005033155

ISBN-13: 978-1-4022-0619-1
ISBN-10: 1-4022-0619-4

Printed and bound in the United States of America
VP 10 9 8 7 6 5 4 3 2

Dedication

To my sisters and best friends, Jane Markota and Carole Wiltfong, whose love and support nourish me always. Growing up was so much fun as we sang, "Sisters, sisters, never were there *three* such sisters," from *White Christmas* at every age and stage of our lives.

Acknowledgments

Any book is a collaborative effort and the result of the talents and efforts of many. I thank all those wonderful Dolphins in my life, past and present, whose contributions enabled me to write this book.

Thank you, Lisa Hagan, my fabulous friend and agent, who read early passages of this work and could always be relied on to give both kudos and feedback. Thanks also to Deb Werksman, perspicacious, talented editor and friend, who has shepherded both my books through the publishing maze and helped me become a better writer. My appreciation to Tara VanTimmeren for her care and final finishing touches.

To Dominique Raccah and all of the wonderful team at Sourcebooks: thank you for believing in my vision and voice, and for asking me to write another book. Sourcebooks is a terrific company and I am proud to be one of your authors.

Thanks to my dad, Mark Campbell, for captaining our wonderful family, and thanks to my sisters, Jane Markota and Carole Wiltfong, and their families—the Markotas: Dick and Robert; the Alwags: Marissa, Max II, and Maxie III; the Dixons: Lindsey and Tyler; and the Wiltfongs: Lloyd, Katie, and Nicholas. Family gatherings are always a swirl of smiles and laughter in my memory.

My sincere love and appreciation to my writers group, Wild Women Writers, Rhonda Britten, Linda Sivertsen, Victoria Loveland-Coen, and especially Carol Allen, my astrologer, who reads and raves and invariably predicts great things. Your loving friendships nurture me and our lunch/brunches always give me great giggles and terrific ideas.

Thanks to the poker girls, Shelley, Barbara, Bobbie, Rita, Trish, Leslie, Diana, and Elyse, for the happy camaraderie of cards, chips, and chatter. You make life fun! And what happens in Vegas stays in Vegas…

To all the Dolphin graduates of the Financial Stress Reduction workshops, all the readers of *The Wealthy Spirit* who sent me their thoughts and blessings, and all my friends past, present, and future, thank you for sharing your stories with me. I treasure all of you.

I wish you all sunny skies, smooth sailing, and treasure ships in your harbors.

Contents

zero
to
zillionaire

Introduction

"Life should not *be a journey to the grave with the intention of arriving safely in an attractive and well preserved body, but rather to skid in sideways, champagne in one hand, strawberries in the other, body thoroughly used up, totally worn out, and screaming, 'Woo hoo—what a ride!'"*

—Unknown

Who am I to be writing this book?

Well, who are you to be reading it?

Please take the following simple test:

1. After you read the title *Zero to Zillionaire,* did you wish the rest of the title read *in 60 Seconds*?

2. Do you think the winner of the Game of Life is the person that dies with the most money in the bank?

3. Do you think success means you have to work eighty-hour weeks?

4. Do you think wealth is a result of the word *work* always being followed by the word *hard*?

5. Are you giving up everything—your family, friends, hobbies, happiness—to secure your financial future?

6. Do you think being open-minded means your brains fall out?

7. Do you believe it is more noble and spiritual to be poor than it is to be rich?

8. Are you trying to start a non-profit organization to help others, even though you don't have enough money to pay your own bills?

9. Do you think the terms *spiritual* and *wealthy* are mutually exclusive?

10. Have you always followed the rules and done what you were told without question? Or always broken the rules, even when the rules made sense?

Hopefully, you answered "no" to all of these questions—except perhaps we all have a secret wish that Zillionaire status could be achieved in sixty seconds. Doing it that fast would be tricky, depending on where you are now on the scale between Zero and Zillionaire and how much further you have to go. But you can be a Zillionaire, and it can happen a lot quicker than you think.

You can be a Zillionaire, and it can happen a lot quicker than you think.

If you answered "no" to these questions, you might already qualify for Zillionaire status: You have an inquiring mind, you care about self-improvement, you read the introductions to books, you are comfortable financially but you want to experience life and not just accumulate things, you care about personal freedom, and you want your life to have meaning. You want wealth in your work, happiness in your home, and a balance between the two. You want a balanced checkbook, a balanced schedule, a balanced spirit, a balanced life.

If you answered "yes" to a few of these questions, you might have some things in your life you'd like to change. You could have lots of money, but not enough time to develop fulfilling relationships. Or you might have a wonderful spirituality and community of friends, but not enough money to keep from worrying about how to pay your bills. Perhaps you've always followed the conventional route, but have a secret longing to throw caution to the wind and strike out on your own in a new venture. Perhaps you have always thrown caution to the wind, but would like your life to be a trifle less wind-swept now. This book will help you balance financial and personal satisfaction in your life: more money, more happiness, more fun, better relationships—in short, more genuine success—by implementing eight successful strategies.

So why did I write this book? What did people need that was missing?

The covers of the business books scream, "Be a Mega Multi-Millionaire!," but what if we don't want to be Bill Gates or Donald Trump or have forty-eight thousand employees—or even forty-eight employees—and all the responsibilities and stresses that go with that? What if we want a business or career that doesn't keep us up nights worrying about how to outrun and outgun the competition? What if we just want a nice, comfortable, upscale life with a job or business that suits us, uses our best skills—and oh, please, God, please, can it be fun, too?

Speaking of God, why did a rich spiritual life and a rich material life seem mutually exclusive? Why did I keep meeting good people who wanted to start charitable foundations but who had no money and had no connections to anyone who had money? And what good did it do those people at Enron and WorldCom to make millions when their legal and ethical violations sent their empires crumbling? The problem I noticed in the world around me was that a lot of the spiritual people were broke, and a lot of the wealthy people had no spirit. Where was the book that balanced the two?

My definition of Zillionaire isn't just about the money. If you have a zillion dollars but no friends, and work that is profitable but isn't fun, you're not a Zillionaire. If you have great friends and fun work but no money, then you're not a Zillionaire, either.

I had created my Financial Stress Reduction workshops in 1990 because so many people seemed to be stressed about money, no matter how much money they had. In fact, a survey reported that of people with more than $10 million in assets, a third of them said money brought more problems than it solved. I knew from the results my participants achieved in the workshops that the eight-week, eight-step format worked. People often told me that when they encountered problems in their lives, they pulled down the workshop workbook from the shelf and reviewed the information. That was the program that I needed to put into book form for my readers. People needed the step-by-step plan for applying the eight strategies I had developed for living life with maximum money, minimum worry, and enlightened enjoyment every day.

My definition of Zillionaire isn't just about the money. If you have a zillion dollars but no friends, and work that is profitable but isn't fun, you're not a Zillionaire. If you have great friends and fun work but no money, then you're not a Zillionaire, either. My definition of Zillionaire is someone who has a zillion dreams of infinite possibility, is taking a zillion actions to make them come true, making as many zillions of dollars as possible, making a zillion friends, doing a zillion good deeds, taking a zillion naps and a zillion vacations, and having a zillion adventures in a long, fun-filled life!

I don't claim to be at the top of the Zillionaire status poll. I am a work in progress myself. But this book isn't as much about attainment as it is about process. Attainment only lasts for a second; process lasts for a lifetime. Why live your whole life in fear that you'll never be Number One, then become Number One and celebrate for a moment, only to live the rest of your life in fear you'll stop being Number One? I don't care what my number is. I'm in the game. I'm on the board scoring points every day towards achieving all the things I want. And I'm having as much fun playing the game as anyone I know.

I'm not one of those advice-givers who has never sat in the loser's chair, never blown an opportunity, never spent money I should have saved or saved money I should have spent. Not only have I been at Zero on the scale, I've been less than Zero. I've lost a house to foreclosure, been mired in six-figure debt, and filed bankruptcy. I've made stupid mistakes, trusted people who weren't trustworthy, invested in foolish schemes, tried wishing instead of working. I looked for answers at the bottom of a bottle. I've been as down and depressed about life and my place in it as anyone.

But I learned from each failure and got up and tried again. Now the Zero days are behind me, and each day I live more and more like a Zillionaire. I have work I love that pays me richly. I have clients I help that praise me generously. I have wonderful hobbies, fabulous friends, and time off to enjoy them. I love my family and they love me back.

I searched out the path and learned how to walk it, all the way from minus-Zero to Zillionaire. I put markers along the way, and I will show you where they are. Now I am living the life I always wanted. It is my design and may not suit you. But I can show you how to design the one *you* want.

Zero to Zillionaire is a scale. We are all on that scale somewhere—some of us are drowning near Zero and some of us are riding the crest of the Zillionaire wave.

Anyone can be a Zillionaire. This book is designed to help move you up the food chain from rags to riches. Think like a Zero and produce Zero results. Think like a Zillionaire and produce Zillionaire results. Wouldn't it be great if the whole world was rich and happy? It begins here. It begins with you.

Strategy 1 | Change Your Mindset and Change Your Future

"Are you ready to give up all hope
of having a better past?"
—Greg Mooers

From Zero to Zillionaire is a scale. Everyone is on the scale somewhere from the lowest to the highest. Why are you where you are? What part of the scale were you born into? Then what did you choose?

Right now, we are thinking and creating our futures. For the most part we do it blindly, unconsciously, without realizing that the habits of thinking that created our past predestine us to more of the same in our future: same job, same boss, same spouse, same house, same money, same religion, same life. A therapist friend of mine, Laura Arnold, asks, "Do you know somebody involved in a relationship with the wrong person—again? Or still?" Just as you must train yourself to think and behave differently in order to choose more fulfilling relationships with people, you will have to think and behave differently in order to choose a more fulfilling relationship with money. Before behavior, there is a thought that produces the behavior. When you think like a Zero, you produce Zero results. In order to be a Zillionaire, you have to think like a Zillionaire.

But first, let's look at what brought us to where we are now. Our Zero or Zillionaire thoughts are rooted in our past.

Carrie's Story

Carrie sobbed as her grandmother Bea shook her.

"How disgusting and evil of you," Bea raged. "Taking advantage of your friends like that. You stole their money!"

"I didn't steal it!" Carrie wailed. "They wanted the candy. I just sold it to them."

"You know that candy was only one cent at the store. You charged them two cents—that's twice as much. You robbed them blind!"

"No, Grandma Bea, I didn't rob them! The candy store closed at six o'clock. I just bought a bunch of candy early so I could sell it to the kids when they wanted it later. I thought I was smart. I thought I could make a little money from it. Isn't that okay?"

The most powerful authority figure in her life had impressed upon her in that wrenching emotional scene that making a profit, especially from her friends, was evil.

"No, no, no! It's not okay to sell one-cent candy for two cents and take advantage of your friends. You are going to give every penny of that ill-gotten money back. I am so ashamed of you!"

Carrie hung her head weeping as Grandma Bea called all the neighbors and told them to come over to the house with their youngsters. Carrie was made to apologize and give back every cent to each child who had bought candy from her. She cried herself to sleep for weeks.

She learned her lesson well: it's a sin to make a profit.

Carrie was still shaken by the memory of that day when she related this story in my workshop. Everyone in the class shook their heads at the power of that bitter lesson. A savvy young business-woman, Carrie had owned her own business for a couple of years. But the most powerful authority figure in her life had impressed upon her in that wrenching emotional scene that making a profit, especially from her friends, was evil.

Every time she had to ask someone for payment, she choked. Every time she felt friendly feelings towards someone (which was pretty much all the time towards everyone), she lowered her prices. She was embarrassed to charge them *any* money, let alone *good* money, for her services. Is it any wonder?

"That's the Story of My Life"

Have you every heard someone say, "That's the story of my life," and they mean their life is joyful, successful, rich, and fabulous? No. It's a euphemism for "My life sucks right now and it always has." It's usually said in a whine.

Do you ever say it? When? Are you acting defeated when you say it? Feeling like a loser? Like a Zero? Do you think people can't tell? They can. You speak it. You reek of it. Your desperate, flailing, losing energy pervades the air and sends up flares like blood in the water summons sharks.

Poker is my hobby. I was playing cards one afternoon when a young fellow walked by and said hello to a man sitting at my table. The man looked up and said, "Hey, Joe, how did you do in that poker tournament last week? When I saw you it looked like you had a mountain of chips in front of you."

"Yeah," the young man smiled. "I did pretty well for a while. I made it to the final table."

"That's great!" said his friend.

But Joe sighed then and shrugged his shoulders. "But I didn't get any good cards after that and I finished in seventh place. I hardly made any money. That's the story of my life."

And all the poker sharks were thinking, Oh, baby, baby, come back and sit right down at my table and play cards with me. Because you're going to lose and I'll be happy to get all that money that you're going to give away!

Contrast that story with this one:

The Texas Hold'em poker jackpot had just been raised to $100,000 during certain hours at the Bicycle Club Casino. The very first day of the big jackpot, a poker player named George announced to each of the floormen that he was going to win it. He told the other players he was going to win it, too. "Isn't that new jackpot great? I'm going to win it today," he repeated over and over.

You know what happened. He won it. People shook their heads muttering about how lucky George was. I overheard a floorman say that George had won six jackpots in the past year, and four the year before that. I introduced myself to him later and inquired if that was true. The truth was even more astounding: the $100,000 jackpot

What is it that makes some people winners and some people losers?

was the fourth jackpot he had won in three days! Yet I know many people who've been playing poker for years who have never won one. And they tell me that sadly, whenever somebody else wins, "I've never won a jackpot. I've never even been at the table when the jackpot's been won. That's the story of my life."

What is it that makes some people winners and some people losers? The clues lie in your past and the stories you tell about your life.

Your Life—Low-Budget Horror Flick or Big, Rich Blockbuster?

What was your life like when you were growing up? Are you in the same financial circumstances now? In the same neighborhood? Did you set your sights higher than your parents or friends or did you get a similar job at a similar pay scale?

Americans hate to think that we have social classes. Rather, we're comfortable with the term *middle class*, but less happy about calling others "upper class" or "lower class." But it is plain to see in every city that we group in socioeconomic milieus. Aside from a few rebellious types who won't follow the norm, most people aspire to blend in with others around them. So there are neighborhoods defined by a high concentration of Blue-Collar/Apartment-Renting/High School Grad/Kmart Shoppers, and others that are home to White-Collar/Tract Home-Owning/College Grad/Nordstrom Shoppers. The fewer rich neighborhoods have Tuxedo-Collar/Mansion-Owning/Grad School Grad/Neiman Marcus Shoppers. My family used to drive by the mansions of Beverly Hills and Pasadena on a Sunday outing. We oohed and ahhed over the gorgeous homes, but no one ever talked about how we might get one for ourselves one day. They were *chimeras*—unattainable dreams to be admired, but not to be had.

If you grow up in a low-rent district, your parents work in low-wage, unskilled jobs, and your friends at school scoff at their studies and have discipline problems, that's most likely what you will do, too. If all the parents on your street are working white-collar dads and stay-at-home moms, it's probable that the majority of the boys on your street are going to go to college and look for professional jobs and middle-class money. The girls are going to do that, too—until they settle down to have a family, if that is the norm of the neighborhood.

We are born into mindsets of expectations that come with their own sets of values, language, and experience. We look around at the people we know, who are like us, and—for the most part unconsciously—we embrace and emulate that picture of our future. It comes with its own set of preprogrammed beliefs—affirming hope or hopelessness, affirming higher education or not, affirming riches or poverty. Some good, some bad, some helpful, some harmful—these beliefs inform our actions, and our actions bind us ever more tightly to the same milieu. We grow up in a box, create more of the same boxes, and, as the song goes, "They're all made out of ticky-tacky and they all look just the same."

> **We are born into mindsets of expectations that come with their own sets of values, language, and experience.**

In the book and movie *Alive*, the true story about the Uruguayan rugby team whose plane crashed in the Andes mountains, only sixteen of the forty-five people on the plane survived to make it out of the mountains seventy days later. Although rescue operations were called off after a short time, some of the parents never gave up hope.

They continued to search for their children, refusing to believe they had perished. The children of those same parents never gave up hope, either, and they were the ones who walked out of the mountains and found help. Parents teach their children with every waking moment how to think and behave, what to expect, and what to value. Their children drink it in and horde it, and that is the reservoir they will draw upon when drought is upon them.

> **Our expectations of our financial futures are laid out for us from the beginning, as we assimilate the luxuriousness or penuriousness of our surroundings.**

In this same way, our expectations of our financial futures are laid out for us from the beginning, as we assimilate the luxuriousness or penuriousness of our surroundings. Our parents' attitudes and beliefs about money filter down and manifest in the quality of our homes, whether we rent or own, where or if we travel, what kinds of things we buy and where we buy them. They manifest in the stories they tell about how hard or easy money is to come by, what is worth spending money on and what is not, whether or not they think they are succeeding in life. When we absorb and repeat the same convictions, without thinking or examining them, they will produce the same results for us.

What is the story about life, success, and money that you were told as a child? Did your parents tell you it was easy to get or difficult? What did they value more than money? Suze Orman, in *9 Steps to Financial Freedom*, recounts how she watched her father run back into the burning conflagration that had been his restaurant. He ran through the flames—not to save a life, but to rescue his cash register. It was blazing hot and burned him badly, but he saved the money. And Suze learned that money was more important than life.

When I speak to groups or teach workshops, I always ask, "Who took a class in school about how to make or manage money?" Very few people raise their hands. So when we're not taught it, we make it up from what is around us. We make it up from what our parents say to us when we're young. We make it up from what our teachers tell us in school. We make it up from the television shows we watch, the newspapers and magazines we read, the stories our friends tell us. We make it up from our milieu. We're all graduates of MSU—Make Stuff Up.

So what have you made up about money? Take some time to reflect about money and the role it has played in your life. Pay attention to your first memory of money. Was it received as a gift or did you earn it? Note your first job—what it was, how much you were paid, whether or not you liked it. Did you ever think of going into business for yourself? If you did, what made you willing to take the risk? If you didn't, what stopped you from taking the risk? Who said, "That's a great idea. Go for it!" and who said, "That'll never work. You'll lose everything if you do that"?

So what have you made up about money?

Write down the financial autobiography of your life. List how many jobs you have had, if they were fun, how much money you made, how much praise and attention you received. What made you leave each job? What enticed you to stay? Did you ask for raises, bonuses, and promotions, or did you wait until they were offered?

Note the patterns of your past behavior and how you chose the amount of money in your life.

This is the financial story of your life. Your choices have been informed by your experience of all that you have seen, heard, felt, recorded in memory, and repeated. We act in accordance with our beliefs, even if we have never examined them. Deep within, you hold cherished beliefs about finances, rich people, wealth, poverty, good, and evil. You were born into a milieu, and your beliefs lock you in the pattern that keeps you in it. Are they facts—or opinions? Are they beliefs—or truths?

Knowledge is power. Self-knowledge is the power to change your future. If we want our outer material life to change, we have to change our inner mental life.

Habits of Thought and Habits of Behavior Produce the Same Old Results

We all naturally have thoughts every day, some positive and some negative. But if we consciously decide to change our thoughts to better quality thoughts, we can change our perception of ourselves, which will change how we behave, which will change others' perceptions of us, which will change our results in life. We can upgrade our thoughts through lifelong education, reading, taking classes, taking risks, and getting some therapy. But along with this, we must discipline our minds to root out the old habits of thinking and develop new ones based on our new learning. The voice of the past is loud and insistent—and habitual. New ideas get lost in the clamor like new seeds get washed away in the rain, leaving alive only the older plants with deep roots. We must discipline ourselves to practice new positive statements while rooting out the

> **We must discipline our minds to root out the old habits of thinking and develop new ones.**

old negative ones, because what we tell ourselves about ourselves, about our world, and about our money is the foundation of our happiness and our prosperity.

I laughed when I heard Cher, in concert at the MGM Grand in Las Vegas, tell a story that began, "So I said to myself, 'Cher...' When I talk to myself, I call myself 'Cher.'" She paused a moment. "Usually, it's followed by 'you stupid bitch.'"

Does that sound familiar? We're all talking to ourselves all the time, and most of it isn't pretty. Studies in neurolinguistic programming have shown that the average human being has around sixty thousand thoughts every day. It's estimated that 95 percent of those thoughts are the same old thoughts we had yesterday. Doesn't that sound about right? Aren't you really familiar with those thoughts you're thinking? You think it's you, but it's not you—it's the voice of your milieu. It's a pre-recorded program on a loop that plays endlessly in your head.

About 80 percent of your thoughts are negative. When I was broke, filing bankruptcy, and losing my home to foreclosure, my everyday thoughts looked like this:

"Chellie, you are such an idiot. How could you be so stupid?"

"Oh, God, another bill—doesn't the mail ever bring anything but bills?"

"You are so broke! You have no money! What are you going to do?"

"This goddamn prospect better sign up today—I need the money or I won't be able to pay my rent, employees, light bill, phone bill..."

"You're going to end up a bag lady, homeless, on the streets."

This is not Zillionaire thinking.

You might think that it was the situation I was in that caused me to think like that, and that those thoughts are appropriate to the situation. Perhaps. We all have "out of the blue" disasters that throw us into a tailspin, that may or may not have been of our own making. I think there are negative thoughts and fears first, which then play out in our experiences. Either way, thinking thoughts like those above won't help your situation or improve your finances. It will only reinforce the negative experience and create more panic and less ability to solve your problems. I knew a man who snarled before every job interview, "Those assholes aren't gong to hire me." Think the interviewers could tell that's what he was thinking? The eighty-pound chip on his shoulder preceded him into the room.

When you're worried, in a panic, and thinking negatively, *everybody knows it*. Desperation is not attractive. Some people are more aware than others and consciously add up the clues. Other people just get a funny feeling that…well, you're just kind of a drag. And then the people who are kind of a drag, too, are the ones who are most attracted to you. Then you all get together and talk about what a drag life is…You see how it works?

You're Wearing Your Thinking

You wear your thoughts like you wear clothes. Your thinking shows up on your face and in your body language and in your energy. You are projecting joy, success, and prosperity or you are projecting misery, failure, and poverty. People can see it and they can feel it. They respond, consciously and unconsciously, to the thoughts you project.

I explained this once on a radio show in Billings, Montanta, when my book *The Wealthy Spirit* was first released. The interviewer was Tommy B, and the call letters of the radio station were KBUL.

Your thinking shows up on your face and in your body language and in your energy.

I pictured him as a skeptical guy in a cowboy hat and boots, and didn't think he was going to be wildly enthusiastic about practicing positive thinking.

I was right. The first thing Tommy said after he introduced me was, "I have to tell you, I am a skeptic. You aren't going to tell me that saying some silly positive phrases is going to make me more money, are you?"

"Well, yes, Tommy, I am," I said.

"Okay," he said, sounding perfectly delighted to have some controversy. "You are going to have to explain how that works."

"It's really quite logical," I explained. "For example, let's say a friend of yours walks into your house and he's really angry about something. Can you tell he's angry before he says so?"

"Yes," replied Tommy.

"What if instead of being angry, he's really happy. Can you tell he's happy before he says anything?"

"Sure," he acknowledged.

"How?" I asked.

"Well, he looks angry, or he looks happy."

"Yes—because you're wearing your thinking. Your emotional state is reflected in your body language and on your face."

"I guess that's true," said Tommy. "But how is that going to make me more money?"

"Wait and I'll explain," I said. "Do you network in the community to promote your radio show? Do you go to Chamber of

Commerce, Rotary Club, and other business or trade associations meetings?"

"Oh, sure," he replied. "I go to things like that all the time."

"When you're there, do you notice that some people look happy and successful, and other people look angry and complaining?"

"Yes," chuckled Tommy.

"And, in addition to promoting yourself, do you sometimes hire the people you meet to provide products or services for you? To design or print your business cards, or sell you stationery supplies, or provide your insurance?"

"Yes."

"So do you hire the people who look happy and successful, or do you hire the people who look angry and complaining?"

"I hire the people who look happy and successful," he replied.

"Why?"

"Because if they look happy and successful, I expect they will do a good job. It will be a pleasure working with them and there won't be any problems."

"Exactly," I said. "That is why positive thinking works. You repeat positive statements to yourself in order to talk yourself into a happy, successful feeling. That feeling is going to show on your face and in your body language. People will look at your smiling face, hear the smile in your voice, and see you as successful. Whether you are or not! In show business they say to 'Fake it 'til you make it.' Positive thinkers are using that principle in daily life. Act joyful and successful every day, and more people will hire you and be willing to pay you top dollar.

Act joyful and successful every day, and more people will hire you and be willing to pay you top dollar.

Soon you'll find you aren't acting anymore. You'll actually be success-ful. And happy. And rich."

"Oh!" exclaimed Tommy. "I never thought about it like that."

We're all wearing our thinking, and other people can tell what it is. The March 2005 issue of *National Geographic* mentioned a classic study by Paul Ekman, a psychologist with the University of California, who conducted an experiment with the isolated Fore people in New Guinea. Although most of them had never seen people from the West before, when they were shown pictures of people with various emotional expressions on their faces, they could easily identify the expressions: anger, sadness, joy, disgust, and fear. Likewise, when Westerners were shown pictures of the Fore wearing these expressions, they had no trouble recognizing the emotions. It is now widely believed that facial expressions reflecting basic emotions are universal.

Most often the job would go to the candidate who has a positive outlook and the confidence and energy to make things happen.

In another study, human resources professionals were asked whether attitude or skills was more important in a job can-didate. They agreed that even if another applicant was more tech-nically qualified, most often the job would go to the candidate who has a positive outlook and the confidence and energy to make things happen. I know that when I owned my bookkeeping firm and placed an ad for prospective employees, I always put, "Computer experience and positive thinking required." That elim-inated all the pessimists—they hated that requirement. Worked perfectly for me.

Think Like a Zero—Produce Zero Results

When I was at the Zero end of the Zero to Zillionaire scale, I had pitiful thoughts about myself and money. I'm sure I was wearing facial
expressions that announced my Zero thinking to the world. What
about you? What are your thoughts about money—the actual statements that you repeat to yourself whenever the word *money* is mentioned? Remember what your parents and teachers said about
money. Is the voice in your head saying the same thing? What did
you learn from your church, synagogue, temple, or other religious or
metaphysical authorities? What are the old clichés about money that
you have memorized and repeated endlessly in your mind? Are they
facts—or just opinions?

Here are some of the thoughts I hear most often from my class
participants:

"Money doesn't grow on trees." (It does if you own an apple
orchard or an orange grove.)

"The love of money is the root of all evil." (This quote is from the
Bible, 1 Timothy 6:9, and is a warning against being obsessive and
putting money above spirituality.)

"A fool and his money are soon parted." (You're afraid you're the
fool, right?)

"There's never enough money." (Actually, Buckminster Fuller's
foundation showed that there is enough wealth in the world for every
man, woman, and child to have a million dollars. However, they also
theorized that if it were all divided and distributed equally, the people
who have all of it now would have all of it again within three years.)

"It's just as easy to fall in love with a rich man as a poor man."
(Not if you're broke. Then you'll only meet other people who are
broke.)

"You can never be too rich or too thin." (Ridiculous. Of course you can be too thin.)

"You have to work hard to make money." (I know lots of people who are working hard who aren't making any money.)

"Money can't buy happiness." (People who say this are usually broke. Funny, but they usually don't look all that happy, either.)

"It takes money to make money." (So if you don't have any, you can give up all hope now? And not have to work to try and improve your lot? A handy phrase used by the resentful.)

"Cold, hard cash." (Ouch. Could we try "warm, friendly moolah" instead?)

Read this list out loud and then take a look at your face in the mirror.

Do you look poor? Fearful? Hungry? Sad or anxious? Do you look angry that life hasn't given you the gifts you deserve? Do you look confident, rich, and happy? If you are wearing your thinking, when the subject of money comes up in conversation, what do you think you look like? Do people read hope for the future or fear of the past on your face?

Think Like a Zillionaire—Produce Zillionaire Results

In her book *Marilyn and Me*, Susan Strasberg recounted how she and Marilyn Monroe were walking in Manhattan one day. Marilyn wore a trench coat, scarf, and sunglasses, and no one took any notice of her. When Susan remarked with surprise at that, Marilyn turned to her and said, "Oh, do you want to see me be 'her'?" Suddenly, her energy shifted, a subtle but dramatic change came over her, and she was immediately surrounded with adoring fans. She had changed her thoughts, which changed her energy, which changed the way people perceived her.

If you want to become a Zillionaire, you have to practice Zillionaire thoughts. Consciously. Out loud. Every day. Because otherwise, the negative thoughts remain your default position, and they keep you a Zero.

This isn't a revolutionary idea, but it amazes me that so many people who know about it still aren't doing it. In *9 Steps to Financial Freedom*, Suze Orman calls these positive thoughts "your new truth" and the press has labeled them "money mantras." T. Harv Eker, in *Secrets of the Millionaire Mind*, calls them "declarations." My friend Rhonda Britten, star of the television show *Starting Over*, calls them "intentions." Affirmations, Zillionations, Schmillionations—I don't care what you call them. Call them "assertions" if you're practical. Call them "affirmations" if you're metaphysical. Call them "Chellie Chants" if you're fun. Call them anything you like. Just call them.

Yeah, yeah—you know all about positive thinking already. I did, too. But knowing about it and practicing it are two different things. When I was teaching Financial Stress Reduction workshops in the early '90s, I noticed I was the most financially stressed person in the room—a rather humbling awareness, as you can imagine. I wondered why all my class participants were creating marvelous financial results for themselves and I wasn't. What were they doing that I wasn't doing?

They were practicing positive statements about money every day. Out loud. I was teaching them, but I wasn't doing them. I was talking the talk, but not walking the walk. Ouch. I thought I was a positive person and knew all that already, so I didn't actually have to *say* positive affirmations—chants, declarations, whatever—anymore, did I? Like, isn't there a time when you're *done*, already?

No. It's irritating, but that's how it is. It's like my dentist who says you don't have to floss all your teeth—just the ones you want to keep. So I started practicing my positive thoughts out loud every day, and in the next six months I doubled my income. And I'm not the only one—I've seen hundreds of people do the same thing.

As long as you're alive, you're still thinking. You're repeating thoughts that make you richer or thoughts that make you poorer.

As long as you're alive, you're still thinking. You're repeating thoughts that make you richer or thoughts that make you poorer. Thoughts that make you happy and thoughts that make you sad. You're doing them now, whether you realize it or not. There's a constant stream of positive and negative statements running through your mind every waking moment.

Affirmations aren't magic words. They are a tool to help you get dressed, to put better emotions on your face, for the viewing public. They help you focus on what's good instead of worrying about what's bad. Worry puts a frown on your face. Confidence puts a smile on your face. Who do you want to work with, frowning people or smiling people?

Let me give you a tip: The more you have repeated the negative statements in your mind, the more awkward and silly it is going to feel to say positive things. As I look around the room when I give speeches, I can see the thoughts of the audience. I see people thinking, Oh, this is great and feels good! And I see other people grumbling, "This is silly and stupid." I notice the guy snoring in the back, and the woman looking thoughtful in the front. I see the happy energy radiating from the faces of the people who know all about this already. I see the desperate people who will try anything, no matter how silly it seems, because they need financial stress reduction and they need it fast.

But this is a book, and I can't see your face. I don't know how you look. But you do. Go look in the mirror and say the usual things you say about money and your life. How happy and successful do you look? Or do you look bitter and twisted? If you want more money, commit now to changing your attitudes about money. Then watch your face change as you practice the following new positive assertions about money:

> **Go look in the mirror and say the usual things you say about money and your life. How happy and successful do you look?**

1. People love to give me money! (Emphasize the word *love*. Relish this one—it's hard to say without smiling!)

2. I am rich and wonderful. (It's not a lie—it's telling the truth in advance.)

3. I am now earning a great big income doing what satisfies me. (State everything in the present tense, not the future—or it's like the sign in the bar that says "Free Beer Tomorrow.")

4. Something wonderful is happening to me today—I can feel it! (Use this one to ramp up your energy and *feel it!*)

5. All my bills are paid up in full and I still have all this money. (All statements must reflect a positive perspective. You want to visualize your bank account overflowing, not overdrawn.)

6. My positive thinking works for me, whether I believe it does or not. (This is for the skeptics, or "realists" as they like to be called.)

7. A lot more money is coming into my life. I deserve it and will use it for my good and others. (You are deserving of life's riches and when you get them, it's really fun to share.)

8. All my clients praise me and pay me! (Isn't that all you want from them? "I love you—and here's some money." Yes!)

9. Money flows to me like water from a faucet! (Just turn on the spigot and money pours in. And put a plug in the sink and bank part of it, too.)

10. Money comes to me easily and effortlessly, waking and sleeping. (Making money while we sleep is what investing is all about.)

11. All my dues are paid in full. (You don't have to "pay your dues" anymore in order to get what you want. You've already paid enough.)

12. Money is rushing to me from expected and unexpected places. (I love to receive money that I've worked for and am expecting, but I want surprise money, too.)

13. I walk, talk, look, act, think, and am rich! (I tried to cover all the bases with this one.)

14. I am a winner—I win often, and I win big! (Take this one with you to Las Vegas, raffles, lotteries, drawings, and prize pools of all shapes and sizes. Besides, you're already a big winner in the lottery of life: You're the one-in-a-zillion sperm that connected with a one-in-a-zillion egg and were born.)

15. I now receive large sums of money—just for being me! (Think of yourself as worthy to receive money. You are!)

16. Thank you, God, for my abundant blessings. (Thank whatever Higher Power you believe in for all that you have. Gratitude is the only thing that studies have *proven* increases happiness.)

17. Every day, I follow my life's design to my heart's desire and I find safe harbor every night. (Promotes your life purpose, happiness, security, and a perfect end to every day.)

One evening as I was teaching my class, I said, "I don't know if billionaires like Bill Gates practice positive assertions like this. Maybe they don't have to. Maybe they were born with wealthy thoughts running through their minds." But a man named Dwyane spoke up right away and said that when he used to work for Bill Gates, he often saw him in the halls saying, "I'm making money. I'm making money..." Since Mr. Gates is way ahead of most of us on the Zillionaire scale, you might want to add that one to your list.

All my dues are paid in full.

If you practice these positive statements every day for twenty-one days, Zillionaire thinking will become a habit. If you aren't even willing to *try* repeating these positive statements, that's what Alcoholics Anonymous calls "contempt prior to investigation." I hand out my list for free everywhere I speak, and it's posted on my website, but most people don't do the statements. And those that do often stop before they get within shouting distance of twenty-one days. Or they do them grudgingly, all the while thinking, This will never work.

Let me give you a tip: if you practice Zillionaire thoughts while skeptically rolling your eyes, sighing, shrugging your shoulders, and giving little self-deprecating laughs, they aren't going to be very effective. If you say them in front of other people who will roll their eyes and tell you that you look ridiculous, you're probably going to stop doing them long before they have a chance of working. If you do them for five minutes a day and the other twenty-three hours and fifty-five minutes you're angry, shouting, sad, depressed, whining, or complaining, you are probably going to see Zero results.

But get started anyway. Do them even if you think they're stupid. Do them even if your life is a mess and you feel broken and hopeless. Use them to talk yourself into *feeling* richer and happier, even before you are. Yes, it's difficult and yes, it feels unnatural. So what? That's what you always feel when you change a habit. Feeling uncomfortable is a sign that you are changing. If you want things outside yourself to change, first you have to change things inside yourself. Otherwise, nothing is going to change.

"Open Sesame!" Open the doors to the treasure house. Open your mind. Open, open, open! Say your Zillionations as if they really were magic words. At the end of three weeks, you might believe they are.

The Placebo's Evil Twin—Nocebo Effects

The placebo effect is when someone is given a harmless sugar pill instead of real medicine, yet they get healthier anyway, just because they *think* they are getting medicine that is making them better. Research has shown that this has a real physical basis: the *expectation of pain relief* activates the body's anti-pain mechanisms—the production of endorphins.

Unfortunately, the placebo effect has an evil twin—the nocebo effect. An article in the *Washington Post* in 2002 stated that people who assume the worst about their health are prone to get sicker. Researchers found that women who believed they were prone to heart disease were nearly four times as likely to die as women with the same risk factors who weren't so fatalistic in their attitudes. The risk of death had nothing to do with their age, blood pressure, or any of the usual culprits, but only with their belief. They could write a new book, *Think and Grow Sick.*

Surgeons hate to operate on people who seem to relish the idea of dying in order to meet with loved ones who have passed away. Herbert Benson, a Harvard professor and the president of the Mind/Body Medical Institute in Boston, stated that "close to 100 percent of people under those circumstances die."

In clinical tests, when participants were warned of side effects, approximately two-thirds of the group reported experiencing the effects they were warned about, even if there was no physical reason for them to do so. In a study in the 1980s, a group was told that an electric current would be passed through their heads and warned that this could cause them to have headaches. After the test, two-thirds of the group reported headaches. But no current had been used! This is just like the stories of Voodoo practitioners who caused someone to sicken and die by the power of their fear that a curse had been put upon them.

The Aviator was a fascinating movie biography of Howard Hughes, and how he suffered from Obsessive Compulsive Disorder (OCD). The DVD contained a clip of a panel discussion of the disease, with star Leonardo DiCaprio, director Martin Scorsese, and Jeffrey M. Schwartz, MD, of the UCLA Neuropsychiatric Institute. Dr. Schwartz stated that "We now know from multiple brain-imaging studies…that when an actor portrays a part, the blood flow in their brain and the serotonin in their brain take on the same characteristics as the actual patient they are portraying." He remarked that even though there are genetic predispositions to disorders like OCD, "we now know the power of the mind to override those signals…We are now in an age where mindful awareness allows us to override the messages from our genome."

If your mind so clearly can affect your health, is it so strange to think that it would affect your bank account? That the expectation of financial woes would likewise affect your brain and cause you to act in ways that would help create the disasters you fear? If mindfulness can overcome genetics, surely it can overcome finances. You will make different financial decisions if you are thinking confidently about your money than if you are fearful. And that often has nothing to do with the reality of how much money you currently have, but rather how much you expect to have in the future. Most people expect their future to coincide with their past—or they are afraid it will. But which past? The negative version or the positive version?

> **If your mind so clearly can affect your health, is it so strange to think that it would affect your bank account?**

Discovering Your Past: Is It Filled with Disasters or Delights?

When you tell the story of your life, is it a balanced viewpoint? Or do you focus on the negative stories or the positive ones? Reread your autobiography and notice which stories you relish the most—"Pitiful Pearl" stories or "Stanley Success" stories.

Now rewrite your history—twice.

The first time, write it from a Zero's perspective and focus on all the bad breaks you ever had, all your accidents and disasters, all the people who were mean to you, hurt or robbed or beat you, and all your financial losses.

When you write the second version, focus on winning. Take pleasure in every good thing that ever happened to you—every win, every success, every raise, bonus, prize, etc. Count all the people who helped you, nurtured you, and loved you.

Both of these stories are true. They are both "the Story of Your Life." But which one do you focus on? Which one shows up on your face? In your body language? Which story do you think about before you go on a job interview, or make a sales call, or go on a date? The story you tell yourself stimulates your mind and body to produce the chemistry of fear or the endorphins of success. From this you create your results—financially, professionally, and personally.

To illustrate, here are some of the things I include in "the Story of My Life":

Version #1: Zero. Lost election for cheerleader. Twice. Was in abusive relationship. Divorced. Failed as an actress—never had a starring role on TV, movies, or Broadway. Was deserted three weeks before wedding. Worked for years as a secretary for little money. Lost major client right after buying out partners from business. Drowned in credit card debt. Bought house at high price, with high-interest mortgage. Couldn't pay bills. Couldn't pay mortgage. Couldn't sell house. Filed bankruptcy. Lost home to foreclosure. Robbed at gunpoint. Attacked in bedroom at 3:00 a.m. Car broken into three times, stolen once. During one eight-month period, mother died, followed by uncle, aunt, cousin's six-month-old baby, and best friend. Abused alcohol. Single. No children.

> **Focus on winning. Take pleasure in every good thing that ever happened to you.**

Don't you just want to say, "Oh, poor thing"? I feel depressed just writing all that. Quick! Version # 2.

Version #2: Zillionaire. Won elections for Pep Club President and Worthy Advisor of Rainbow Girls. Leading roles in school plays. Won Outstanding Senior Speech Arts Award. Graduated Magna Cum Laude from UC Santa Barbara. Selected Outstanding Senior in Drama Department. Worked often and had great fun in professional acting career—member of Screen Actors Guild, Actors Equity, and AFTRA. Found new career in bookkeeping service, grew business from $80,000 annual sales to $420,000 annual sales in four years. Made partner, then bought business. Saved business after loss of big client. Invented new business— Financial Stress Reduction workshops. Elected President of L.A. Chapter of National Association of Women Business Owners, won Small Business Administration Women in Business Advocate award, Pacific Palisades Rotarian of the Year, Women's Referral Service Member of the Year, Women in Management Most Inspirational Speaker. Got sober, happy, joyous, and free. Make six-figure income. Author of two published books. Have fabulous friends and family. Enjoy every day—making money, having fun, and helping people.

Same life, different perspective. Both versions are true. But if I allow myself to think about the Zero version each day before I make a phone call or write an email or go to a meeting, I'm going to be depressed. That's going to show. Then, if I call you and you're a Zillionaire, you're going to be put off by the negative undertone you feel from me. Conversely, if you're a whiner and complainer Zero, you're going to be ever so attracted to me. If I think about the negative version of "the Story of My Life," I'll be unconsciously repeating negative thoughts all day long. But if I think about the positive version, I'll be happy and the successful people will be the ones most drawn to me.

Throughout my life, when I focused on Version #1 and all my sad stories, I created more sad stories to tell. I am loathe to admit it, but for long periods I was a "Pitiful Pearl." I got an emotional charge out of how unfair life was, how great I was to keep struggling against all odds, and how strong I was to be a survivor, and I loved the "Oh, poor things" people comforted me with.

But those weren't the rewards I wanted in life. "Oh, poor things" weren't paying my rent or sending me on Mediterranean cruises. One day I looked at "the Story of My Life" and I wanted a different story. I wanted different results. I wanted success, and money, and vacations. The good story was there all along—I just hadn't been focusing on it. And when I changed the story I told myself and told others, I changed the course of my future. Better jobs came my way, along with better friends. I started saving money, yet always seemed to have enough to buy the things I wanted and take vacations, too. I quadrupled my income.

> **One day I looked at "the Story of My Life" and I wanted a different story. I wanted different results. I wanted success, and money, and vacations. The good story was there all along—I just hadn't been focusing on it.**

Which story are you focused on? What are your results? If you have more of what you don't want, you're thinking Version #1. If you have what you do want and are getting even more, you're thinking Version #2.

People often ask me for specific statements to solve specific problems. "Can you give me a prescription for procrastination, Chellie?" they ask. I can. "Do you have special affirmations for getting past writers block?" I do. "How do you get so lucky at cards?" I'll never tell.

But you can do this on your own. Just take a piece of paper and draw a line vertically down the center of it. On the left, write down all your current thoughts about your situation, however awful they are. After you've written everything you can think of, on the right hand side, write the exact opposite of all the negative statements as a positive, like this:

Negative	Positive
"I can never seem to meet deadlines."	"I always finish tasks long before they are due!"
"I can't think of anything to write."	"My writing flows easily from my spirit to the page."
"I never have any money."	"I always have plenty of money."
"I hate my life."	"I love my life."

Change your thoughts, change your money, change your life.

Strategy 2 | Choose the Goals That Make You Rich

"Our plans miscarry because they have no aim. When you don't know what harbor you're aiming for, no wind is the right wind."
—Seneca

I wear gold tennis shoes. Always. I have gold leather tennis shoes for regular wear, gold mesh tennis shoes with rhinestones for speaking engagements, and gold-beaded tennis shoes for black tie affairs. All gold tennis shoes, all the time.

At first, I only wore them for fun. Then one year I gave up high heels for Lent, and I haven't had them on my feet since. I decided that being comfortable and cute in my own way—not in the fashion industry way—makes me a Zillionaire. I am always comfortable and my feet never hurt. That makes me happy, and happiness is a Zillionaire trait. You will know Zillionaires by their smiles.

What do you really want? Not what you think you should want, or what your parents said you should want, or what your spouse, your partner, your friend, magazines, or television says would be a great thing to want. Zillionaires are aware of the inner core values that are important to them, and their outer lives reflect them. Inner core value: comfort. Outer reflection: gold tennies.

But what if you don't know what you want? At one point in *Alice in Wonderland*, Alice was walking through the woods when suddenly the path she was walking on diverged in two different directions. Confused, she stopped, not knowing which path to take.

At that moment, the Cheshire Cat appeared in the tree next to her. She asked him which way she should go. "Where are you going?" he inquired.

"I don't know," she replied.

"Then it doesn't matter which path you take, does it?" said the Cat, and disappeared.

If you don't know where you're going, any path will take you there. Tell me what you want and I can help you locate the right port and help you navigate your ship into that port, and the Universe will kick in the right breeze to lift your sails. But no one knows how to help you get to "I don't know."

> **If you don't know where you're going, any path will take you there.**

Pick a goal. Any goal. Your best guess for today will do. Don't wait for the right goal or the perfect goal. It may be around the bend in the road and you can't see it from where you stand today. Pick an interim goal that will get you in action, give you experience in achieving goals, and one day you'll find yourself around that bend where your "perfect goal" is within reach after all.

Here are some questions to guide you: How much money do you want to make? What job do you want to do that pays that kind of money? Think about what your talents and skills are, and what you most enjoy doing. Who are the people who need what you have and would pay you for it? Decide whether you want to work for someone else or own your own business, whether you want to work as part of a team or alone as a sole practitioner.

If your fondest desire is to own your own business, how big would you like it to be? Do you want to serve many customers or just a few? Choose whether you want to be a hair stylist or own a chain of beauty salons. Choose whether you want to be a personal trainer or own a gym. Or a chain of gyms. If you want to manufacture a product, choose how many. Do you want to lovingly handcraft fine cabinets yourself, or do you want to mass market furniture? Do you want to be a sole practitioner accountant or develop a giant multi-national firm like the Big Four? Do you want a job, a career, a profession, or a calling? What moves you, motivates you, inspires you? What gets you up in the morning with a smile and an "I can hardly wait"?

Children are masters of "I can hardly wait." They are laser-focused when they decide they want something. They want it all and they want it now. And they "can hardly wait" until the day when they get it.

When my nephew Robert was four years old, both of his older sisters were on T-ball teams. They had bright, crisp uniforms and practiced every week. When game day came, the whole family sat in the bleachers and cheered them on. More than anything else, Robert wanted to play T-ball.

But there were no T-ball teams for four-year-olds. The minimum age was five. Mama Jane patiently explained this to him every time he watched his sisters play. "Okay, I'm going to play T-ball, too," Robert said. "Just as soon as I'm five. I can hardly wait!"

Then one warm Spring afternoon, Jane, Robert, the two girls, and their dad went to the neighborhood park. There were several families there already, and they had started a pick-up game of T-ball.

Laughing, the girls and their parents ran out on the field to join in the fun. But Robert stayed behind.

Jane turned around and saw Robert on the sidelines looking dejected.

"Come on, Robert," she called, "you can play with us today!"

"No, I can't," said Robert.

"Yes, you can!" Jane exclaimed. "Today you can play."

"I can?" Robert asked, wide-eyed with excitement. "Am I five?"

Today, let's all be five. Let's play T-ball, or basketball, or tennis, or poker, or Wheel of Fortune. Let's join a group and play a game for all we're worth. Play the Game of Life for all we're worth. It's the only game in town, and the only way to lose is not to play, crying, "I don't know what I want."

Bigger Games Have Bigger Price Tags

With my bookkeeping service, my goal was to build a big business, which meant I had to build a big fleet of ships. Over the course of several years, I had the experience of running a business, having thirteen employees in my bookkeeping business and hundreds of clients, being president or on the board of directors of organizations—and working eighty-hour weeks. I knew the financial stress of needing every client to pay on time in order to meet payroll. I knew the importance of working "on" my business and not "in" my business, as Michael Gerber says in *The E-Myth*. When I did bookkeeping myself, I was limited to the number of hours I myself could work each week. But if I focused on building a company and bringing in clients, I could hire as many bookkeepers as I needed to do the work I brought in. I decided I wanted a big business.

But I burned myself out. I worked too hard for too many hours. I struggled with the stresses of funding the growth of the business, overseeing employees to make sure they had the talents and skills to do the work properly, motivating them, helping them build their skills, rectifying mistakes when they occurred, handling turnover, keeping time sheets, overseeing the billing, estimating cash flow projections, handling employee and customer problems, and all the tasks inherent in business ownership. I worried about collections, taxes, government regulations, and the staff member who was making unwanted advances to the girl working in our sublet office. I worried about the fact that we couldn't charge as much for bookkeeping services as an accountant or attorney could charge for their services, yet all my costs for rent, phone service, printing, taxes, etc. were the same as theirs. I finally realized my business model just wasn't profitable…at least not the way I was doing it.

When I was president of the Los Angeles Chapter of the National Association of Women Business Owners, I spoke with a Vice President of Sales and Marketing at Disney, who told me he was in the market for a business to buy. "What kind of business?" I asked. "It doesn't matter what kind," he answered. "Running a business is running a business. The tasks are the same, no matter what kind of business it is. I'm looking for a three- to five-million-dollar business."

Running a business is running a business. The tasks are the same, no matter what kind of business it is.

I often pondered that conversation, and reviewed my goals and my life's path. After a career as an actress, I had landed a job in a bookkeeping service and then was promoted to manager. I started growing the business because that was the next logical step. When the owners of the business made me a partner, the entrepreneurial light bulb went on and I took on that role. Eventually, I bought my partners out, and continued to grow the business. When we lost our biggest client and the business was floundering, I set about rebuilding. But it was slow and hard. I was very financially stressed. And I didn't love it.

It was time to change goals. What did I love? What was I good at? What was my life's purpose? What service could I offer people that they wanted and needed? What empowered my life and at the same time empowered others?

I knew what it was. The workshop business I had developed as a sideline to my bookkeeping service was perfect for me. I loved teaching people about business, sales, goal-getting, networking, money management, overcoming obstacles, achieving balance, perspective, profit, and purpose. I was passionate about coaching people to go for their goals and reach for the stars, yet be content if they only got the moon, and live a happy life.

I wanted those goals for myself, too. As I struggled with building my business, I kept meeting people in the business community who looked relaxed and serenely happy. Contented. Over and over, these people would tell me that they used to own a big business, too. But they were working too hard and not having enough time to enjoy their lives and their families. So, they made a new choice, sold their businesses, and became consultants working out of their home.

At first, I couldn't imagine why someone would want to give up their big dreams and work from home. I had a snotty attitude about it. I felt that people working from home must be deficient in some way—unable to get ahead, build their business, or make more money.

In the beginning of the working-from-home movement, home-based businesses didn't get much respect. Not having an office didn't look professional to me. But contentment shone from the faces of the home-based entrepreneurs—and they seemed to be pretty well-off financially, too. Hmmm. My goals started shifting.

I wanted what they had. I wanted to be happy. I wanted a Chellie-sized business. My workshop business was popular, and it was fun. It was also a low-overhead/high profit business. All I needed were participants, a room, workbooks, and a telephone. I went to work every day and sat with my goals every night. It was clear I had the perfect business for me sitting in my lap. But I was afraid. How did I give up the business management company I had devoted myself to for twelve years? How did I give up my employees and clients with whom I had worked for so long?

Mind you, I was quite brilliant at convincing the participants in my workshops to quit *their* day jobs and go for *their* dreams. Some of them were beginning to look at me quizzically, commenting, "Yeah, Chellie, what about you? What are you doing with that book-keeping service? Why don't you get rid of it and just teach the classes? Teaching these workshops is what you love."

I was afraid, of course. The bookkeeping service was my day job and it paid the rent. When I made a sale with a bookkeeping client, they were mine for years, and sent me a regular check every month. Just like a job. With the workshop business, I had to sell new people workshops every eight weeks. I recognized that there was going to be a lot more emphasis on sales in my daily routine in this business. What if I couldn't do that? What if it didn't work out? What would I do then? I sat in my indecision and waited for a sign.

It wasn't long in coming.

You Can Wait for a Sign Until It Falls on You

Dr. Gary was my number one client and had been with my company since the day I had started twelve years before. But now, he said, "Chellie, I'm transferring my business to someone else. You've lost your interest in this business and I feel you've lost your interest in me." I was saddened by his call—embarrassed, too, because he was right. I had to acknowledge the truth. His call looked like bad news but it was really good news. It was the sign I had asked for, although it was a pink slip rather than an engraved invitation to a party. He gave me permission to change dreams. I put the bookkeeping service up for sale.

It looked like bad news but it was really good news.

At the time I made this decision, I didn't know if I could enroll enough people week after week and month after month to make a living in a workshop business. I wasn't Tony Robbins, I didn't have a big organization, I wasn't on television infomercials every night of the week. But copying Tony Robbins wasn't my vision, anyway. I no longer wanted a big business. I wanted a small one. I wasn't sure it was possible. But then, you never know if you can do things before you do them. I knew I had to go for it. I sold the bookkeeping service to a local CPA and plunged into the workshop business full-time.

I felt like I had been let out of jail.

My spirit soared. I was excited every day I woke up and started work! Suddenly, with the workshop business, my career path finally made sense. In a former period of my life, my only goal had been to be a working actor. I loved every minute of it…right up to the point when I didn't love it anymore. I performed a show at Disneyland five shows a day, five days a week for nine months, and after about six weeks, I was bored out of my skull. When I did *Hello, Dolly!* with Martha Raye, the leading actor playing Cornelius had been playing Cornelius eight shows a week for three years. I was not thrilled. In all my training throughout school, we always had short, four- to six-week runs in plays, and then we'd jump into a new show. That was not the way it was for a professional, where a long run meant you were a successful, working actor. I began to reevaluate my choice of career.

And then one day, I just didn't want to go on one more audition, talk to one more agent, get my photographs taken one more time. I didn't want to have another conversation about the audition I had or what part I was "up for." I no longer loved the daily to-dos of being an actor. Meanwhile, I was working as a secretary between acting jobs, and they promoted me to Office Manager. That involved bookkeeping, which I knew nothing about. But I took the risk to try it and discovered—who knew?—that I loved bookkeeping. It was figuring out how to make money and how best to distribute it. That was fascinating to me, and I switched careers. From actress to bookkeeper—I didn't understand how these two widely divergent professions made sense in my life.

But when I started teaching workshops, suddenly the fractured pieces of the jigsaw puzzle of my life came together, and from all the dots of color the picture emerged. As an actor, I had developed the performing skills I needed to be a professional speaker and present seminars. As a bookkeeper, I had developed the subject matter to speak about. It seemed to me that all my life, I had been in training to deliver the Financial Stress Reduction workshops. It was my "one-woman show" about money. And then I wrote a book about it and then another...

Creating a Life While Creating a Living

You create your life while you're busy creating your living. Each "way leads on to way" as Robert Frost said in *Two Roads Diverged in a Yellow Wood*. As we choose one road and turn our backs on the other, the scene shifts, different people appear, and a different life is lived. Each new choice leads us to a different place, a different scene, a different awareness. It is our goals that inform our choices, and lead us onward to a hoped-for outcome, some of which are realized and some that are not. Along the way, things happen that we could not have expected. The goal is the destination that keeps us moving west or east or sideways on life's 101 Freeway. Each roadside exit we pass is a possible future lost. Each freeway off ramp we choose leads us down a different path to an alternate reality and some other future.

In the 1960s, Marta Becket and her husband were driving across the California desert when their car broke down in a little town called Death Valley Junction. In this small, dusty, out-of-the-way hamlet, with few buildings and fewer people, Marta's artist's eyes lit on a crumbling and deserted opera house. She was at the tail end of her dancing career—but she didn't feel finished. She looked at that theater and new possibilities engaged her creative mind.

She bought the theater. The nearest town was twenty-five miles away and there wasn't a ready-made audience for whom she could easily perform. She performed anyway. For years, no one came. She painted an audience on the walls—it took her six years—and performed for them. Eventually, word of this unusual artist spread throughout the West. Now, eighty-something Marta completely sells out every performance. *Amargosa*, Todd Robinson's documentary film about her life, completely enthralled me with its tale of how this brave, original artist made a life out of dry dust, adobe, and grit in a place no one expected.

This is the Processional Effect in action. The goal you choose gets you on the freeway from Point A to Point B. But somewhere before you get to Point B, you arrive at Point X. This is the place where the road diverges and you stare down the path to a new possibility. Should you stay the course, ignore the new idea, and keep to the original plan? Or should you change your mind, shift gears, turn left, and follow the new road with its neon sign promising "Gas/Food/Lodging"?

What informs your choice is the goal within the goal—the things you really want that you think you will get if you achieve your outer goal. I wanted to be an actress, Marta wanted to dance and paint—those were the outer goals. But the goals within were that we wanted creative expression and independence. We both like applause—every performer does—and that's an outer goal. But the inner goal is that receiving applause means we have touched people and so perhaps we are loved.

> **The goal you choose gets you from Point A to Point B. But somewhere before you get to Point B, you arrive at Point X. This is the place where the road diverges and you stare down the path to a new possibility.**

My outer goals included making good money and having nice things, traveling, learning, exploring the world. Inner goals were that I wanted to be creative and have fun; I wanted friendships and laughter. And I wanted to do some good in the world. I wanted to make a difference. The outer goal is the means we choose to quench our inner thirst for meaning in our lives.

The goal within is the one that our soul needs to flourish. It is our deepest yearning to live a good life, be a good person, be connected, and be loved. It is wrapped up in the outer goal like a perfectly packaged present, with bright colored paper, tied with a gleaming gold and crimson bow. But it's no use putting gilded ribbons on a parcel full of stones and coal—we've all seen people who have the gift wrap done perfectly but are miserable little lumps inside the box. And we've seen beacons of light and goodness shining through wrappings that are dull and poorly taped together. The outer goal is the gift wrap; the inner goal is the gift—don't confuse the two.

A Zillionaire does the work necessary to make both the inner and the outer goals shiny and bright. When you choose your goals, and decide on a road to take you there, make sure that the inner goal will be nourished by the outer goal you have chosen. What kind of a life do you want? What kind of business or job will get you that? What are you willing to do, learn, and be in order to have it?

> **A zillion studies have shown that people who write down their goals are more successful than people who don't. Have you written yours?**

A zillion studies have shown that people who write down their goals are more successful than people who don't. Have you written yours? No, you can't just think about them. You have to write them. It's a Zillionaire requirement. Knowing about it and doing it are two separate things. When you write your goals, you are starting the process of bringing what you want from metaphysical reality (thoughts, dreams, and wishes) to physical reality (actual material results). Go to your computer or get a piece of paper and start scribbling—what do you really want? Let's create all those things you want instead of wishing you had them or resenting someone else who has them.

You Are the Star of Your Movie

You are the star of the movie of your life. You write the script and you direct it. You hire the supporting actors, you design the sets and the costumes, you gather the props. You do the location scouting, and you're in charge of transportation. You are your agent and manager, too: did you negotiate a big enough salary, bonus, perks? Now, action! The camera is on you, baby! What do you want *the Story of Your Life* to be about?

Create your ideal movie scene by following these guidelines:

1. Describe your ideal home. What style of architecture is it? English Tudor, Spanish hacienda, ultra-modern multi-level? Is it in the country or the city? By the ocean, on a mountain, or in the suburbs? Stand in front of it and look. See your front door in your mind's eye, walk up to it, open the door, and walk in. Picture the interior design and furnishings. What are the colors, textures, light, energy, smells inside your home?

2. Next, look at your ideal neighborhood. Are you friends with your neighbors? Do you borrow each other's sugar and lawnmowers? Do your kids play together? Do you have block parties in the street? Notice who you love and who loves you.

3. From your neighborhood, enlarge your vision to your ideal place of work. Picture the kind of work are you doing. Do you have a boss, associates, partners, employees? Or do you work alone? What kinds of tasks are you doing in your work, and what tasks are being done by others? Write down your achievements, awards, and recognition. Do you travel for your work? Where? Notice

what brings you joy in your work and who you are helping and serving.

4. Enlarge your vision again, and see yourself in your community. Notice how you are connected with the people with whom you live and work. Do you belong to a church, synagogue, temple, or other spiritual group? Are you a member of a union, trade organization, or professional association? Describe your involvement in politics, hobbies, social clubs, etc. What are you doing for fun and who are you doing it with?

5. Lastly, notice your connection to the world. Do you travel to foreign countries? Do you participate in philanthropic organizations? Do you donate time and money to charities? Are there still crystal clear oceans and clean air? Describe the part you play in the world game.

What part of this vision can you accomplish in one year? At the top of a sheet of paper, write "Zillionaire Goals I will accomplish by _____" and write in the date one year from today. Then write another list of goals that will be accomplished in five years. State your goals as if they are already accomplished, like this:

"I am now making $300,000 per year easily and effortlessly, doing the work I love."

"I am taking a fabulous vacation cruise to the Mediterranean Sea for fourteen days and I am having a wonderful time!"

"I own a fabulous house that is a money-making investment, too!"

And because being a Zillionaire means having a balanced life with meaningful relationships, add goals like these:

"I radiate perfect health—mentally, physically, and spiritually."

"I am a beautiful and loving person."

"I maintain loving, harmonious relationships with all my family and many friends."

Dream big! Add some goals that are a stretch for you, that make you laugh and your eyes shine when you think about actually achieving them. Just the pursuit of them can be thrilling. Why not go for it? You might be surprised what shows up in your life—sooner than you expected.

For example, I admire the lavish high-roller suites maintained by the Las Vegas hotels for their "whales"—the gamblers who wager millions of dollars in their casinos. The rooms are gorgeous, filled with the richest fabrics and elegant furniture—and a butler to do their bidding. The high-rollers are waited on hand and foot, and their every wish is granted. Chellie is not a whale at this point, but still, I put "I spend the night in a fabulous high-roller suite" on my list of goals.

> Why not go for it? You might be surprised what shows up in your life— sooner than you expected.

I forgot all about it the next month as I jetted off with three of my girlfriends for a cruise on a paddlewheel steamer up the Mississippi River from New Orleans to Memphis. We were staying in New Orleans to take in the sights for a couple of days before getting on our ship, the Mississippi Queen.

As we waited in line at the check-in counter at the Intercontinental Hotel in New Orleans, the harried clerk apologized profusely—they were completely overbooked. The rooms we reserved weren't available. She asked if we would mind sharing a suite instead of having separate rooms. We said, "Sure!" because we're easygoing people, and we were on vacation and having fun.

We thought it would be fine and dandy to share living quarters rather than be separated into two rooms.

"Okay, then," said the clerk, "but I have to tell you the suite only has one bed in each of the two bedrooms, so we'd have to bring in a rollaway for each of you. Sorry about that."

We shrugged, and said that would be fine.

"You're sure that's okay? We're so sorry for the trouble," apologized the clerk.

"Really, it's fine, okay, no problem," we chorused.

We knew something good had happened when we had to use our key in the elevator to get to the concierge floor. Hmmm. We smiled at each other as we alighted on the top floor and passed the lovely room where they served complimentary munchies and soft drinks. Down the hall we went to the last door, and opened it slowly.

Our collective breaths caught as we saw the black-and-white marble-tiled floor of the entryway and the full-length oil painting and large vase of flowers. This was no ordinary suite. We dropped our bags on the floor and turned right into the living room. It was huge! Fireplace, couches, television, elegant tables and chairs, a dining table set for ten in the dining room, and a full kitchen behind that. The balcony alone was bigger than the usual hotel room. We discovered a small den, with a wet bar and another television. The master bedroom was huge, with a gorgeous four-poster bed, and the master bath had a whirlpool bathtub and another television. The second bedroom was smaller, but still fabulous. We were jumping up and down with "oohs" and "ahhs" as we explored our very own Fit-for-a-Zillionaire high-roller suite. We took turns sprawling on the living room couch and lounging in the bathtub watching TV. We had such fun, it was hard to tear ourselves away and explore the city.

We had been given a free upgrade to the Presidential Suite that goes for $2,000 a night! And I had put "stay in a high-roller suite" on my list of goals only one month before.

Live it up! What secret goal do you want but are afraid to name because you can't see how you would ever get it, how you would qualify for it? Want to put high-roller suite on your list even if you're not a high-roller? Or an overnight stay at Buckingham Palace, even if you're not royalty? Or free front-row seats at the next Bon Jovi concert with a backstage pass, even if you don't have "connections"?

Go for goal, Zillionaire!

You Can "Yeah, but..." Your Way to Zero

Every day you don't take action to achieve your dreams is a day you are creating more of what you have right now. If what you have now is perfect, then you only have to take the same actions to continue to maintain it. Great. But then don't tell me you're life isn't what you want. If you're complaining about the way things are without taking any steps to change it, you're likely to end up being one of the "Ain't It Awful" people who are constantly whining about the price of gasoline, or taxes, or houses, or the weather, the traffic, the kids these days, television commercials, their spouse, the neighbors, and email spam. (Like there's something you can do about *that*.)

> **If what you have now is perfect, then you only have to take the same actions to continue to maintain it.**

As my friend, author Eddie Connor, says, "Let me kick you in your 'but.'" Stop sniveling and move on. No one cares about how rocky the coastline is or how bad the storms were or how long you studied navigation or how the crew mutinied or how abused you were or how hard it is to sail a ship. They just want fun ports, lots of food, and good shopping on their cruise.

You're too old? Grandma Moses was eighty-five when she started painting masterpieces. Colonel Sanders was sixty-five when he got his first social security check, said to himself, "This will never do," and started Kentucky Fried Chicken. I started writing my first book at age fifty and it was published when I was fifty-four. So you're too old and it's too late for you to do—what? One of my friends told me everyone knew her acting career was over because she was forty years old, and I rolled my eyes and said the showbiz types had been telling that old lie forever but that didn't make it true. She gaped at me—she had never thought to challenge that idea. It was accepted wisdom in her industry. I told her to do her research and she would discover just how many actresses became successful *after* age forty. She had never thought to investigate, but when she did, she came up with a list of seventy-five women.

> There is one "Yeah, but" that is permissible: you do have to acknowledge what your gifts are and not what you wish they were.

There is one "Yeah, but" that is permissible: you do have to acknowledge what your gifts are and not what you wish they were. If you want to sing professionally, you should be able to carry a tune. If you want to be an NBA star, it would be a good thing if you were tall and nimble with a ball. If you want to be a supermodel, it's helpful if you're thin and beautiful. That's not to say there aren't exceptions that disprove the rule, but it helps to put the odds in your favor.

You can't "positive think" your way into a talent you don't possess. An hour of watching *American Idol* on television should convince you of that. No one is served when you tell your friend or family member that they sing like Clay Aiken, when they really sound more like William Hung. But then again, William got a record deal, too. If you weren't born with the talent to sing extraordinarily well, accept it. By all means, still sing—sing for the joy of singing, sing for the communion of voices when in a group like at church, sing happy songs in the shower to start your day on an upbeat note. But don't waste your life pursuing a dream of being a famous pop singer, when really your best talent might be to help the sick and dying by running a hospice. We are all born with gifts. Some are dynamic and bright and shine like comets in the night sky. Some are quiet and soft, like moonlight on a meadow. Your mission is to find your passion, what makes your life sing, and then sing that song for all you're worth. Your song will be different from everyone else's song, and therefore special, unique, and wonderful. Don't try to sing someone else's life song. It can't be copied. I can sing a perfect Chellie Campbell but only a second-rate Bette Midler.

Big and Powerful Versus Small and Happy

I've been happy as a poker player with a straight flush with my little workshop business—helping people, getting kudos, and getting paid. I hold my workshops in the den at my house. I put the coffee on, twelve people show up, I teach them, they go home, I turn the coffee off. I love my income. I love my overhead. I love my commute. I love my life.

T. Harv Eker is the president of Peak Potentials Training. He's in the workshop business, too. He has a big vision, a big company, and he's making big money. His game plan is masterful—he contacts the presidents of various networking groups and offers free passes to his Millionaire Mind Intensive three-day seminar for each member of their group. They do Harv's marketing for him by advertising this wonderful free benefit to their membership. It's a classic win-win-win scenario: Harv wins, the organization wins, and the members win. Brilliant.

So I got my free pass and I went to the seminar. There were some twelve hundred people at the one I attended. For three days, Harv gave an informative, fun, involving seminar. "You have a Millionaire Mind!" Everyone high-fived each other on cue. And for three days, from eight o'clock in the morning until ten at night, he sold you—masterfully—the next ten programs that you are going to need if you are *really* committed to improve your money and your life. The programs come with high price tags—I remember one was $3,995—but then he gives you a big discount because he really cares about you and wants to help. So he slashes the price to $2,995, throws in the $1,000 CD set for free along with it, and then discounts the whole price again. But you have to take advantage of this offer right now, because this course is almost sold out and he only has fifty spaces left...

Need I tell you that hundreds of people jumped up out of their seats and ran to the back of the room to give the waiting employees their credit cards? Because they "have a Millionaire Mind!" And Harv has a Millionaire Bank Account. He told us he makes over a million dollars a weekend. Fabulous. I was watching a master at work. I saw what was possible when your vision was huge.

Then he wrote a book, *Secrets of the Millionaire Mind*. It has a big sticker on the front that says "Free bonus—Two tickets to the Millionaire Mind Seminar, Worth $2,590—Details Inside." Inside the book, there's a coupon and instructions how to use it. Throughout the book, he says, "…and if you attend the Millionaire Mind Intensive Seminar, you will dramatically accelerate your progress" and "that is exactly what we will continue to do in Part II of this book and do even further with you at the Millionaire Mind Intensive Seminar." There are many, many references to his seminar in his book, because if you come to the free seminar, you are quite likely to buy the other seminars, and he makes a lot more money from the $2,000+ seminars than he docs from the small percentage an author is paid on the $19.95 price of a book. The book is just one piece of direct marketing material.

Do you think I sound jealous or sad that my business is so much smaller than his? Well, I admit I wasn't too fond of him in the beginning when one of my favorite networking groups started touting his financial seminar from the podium every meeting and not mine. He was Oz, the Great and Powerful, and I was Dorothy, the Small and Meek. Was my vision too small, I wondered? Should I be doing what he's doing? (I hate it when I *should* on myself.) But I got over that. Some people would rather come to me and sit with twelve people in a living room for eight weeks than go to a hotel and sit with twelve hundred people for three days. Some will prefer personal attention over mob psychology. I will always find "My People." Harv will always find his. You will always find yours. There's no such thing as competition.

Listen, my hat's off to Harv. He's figured out a great program and a way to sell it that is gangbusters. I believe he's helping a lot of people with his programs, too. I think you should go to his free seminar, if only to see these kinds of sales techniques in action. (And tell him I sent you—my ambassador code is 108029. I'll get a commission, by gum.) Harv is a master of the big picture seminar business, like Tony Robbins and Werner Erhard before him. Hey, if you want that big picture, go ahead and get it. Have forty-eight or forty-eight hundred employees. Get twenty-five thousand emails a day. Train thousands of people. If that's what you want, if that's what Zillionaire means to you, then go for it. It's your movie and you can write the script any way you want.

I'm more like comedian Steven Wright, who said, "Ambition is a poor excuse for not having enough sense to be lazy. Hard work pays off in the future, laziness pays off now." The Big Blockbuster Movie isn't my movie. I am too aware of the big price one pays for the big picture. T. Harv Eker names it in his book:

Are you willing to work sixteen hours a day? Rich people are. Are you willing to work seven days a week and give up most of your weekends? Rich people are. Are you willing to sacrifice seeing your family, your friends, and give up your recreations and hobbies? Rich people are.

No, non, nein, no, no. Nope. Not me. Not willing to pay. If you want the big goal, good for you. Be my guest. Go read one of the big boys' books and try and win the rat race. But make sure you take a good squint at the price tag for that life, too. The big vision doesn't come cheap.

Sign me up for the Small Independent Film, the smaller vision, the smaller goal, and the smaller price, thanks. I don't have ten workshops, I just have one. One workshop that works is all I need. I say what the price is and that's the price all the time for everybody. I purposefully did not create a business—I created a job for myself. And I'm not alone—there are 17.5 million of us solo-preneurs in the

There are 17.5 million of us solo-preneurs in the United States.

United States. The ads say, "Go big or go home." Bah. We already are home. With work we love, cash in our pockets, and family around us—happy, rich enough, and fulfilled.

The downside is that when you just create a job for yourself, it is totally dependent on you, and without you it ceases to exist. So I think about Harv's model and my model. And when my friend Michelle Anton calls me up and says, "The next level for you, Chellie, is to train other people to lead your workshops. Here's your two-million-dollar plan: you do two trainings a year with one hundred people, at ten thousand dollars a person," I listen. That game plan would shift my focus from training individuals to training trainers. I could still work on a scale small enough to suit me and yet increase the reach of my work through others.

> Every time I examine my business and whether or not to expand, I filter everything through my goal within the goal: I want to be small and happy and rich.

I may do it. I am ruminating about it. But first things first: today I have to write this book. I'm putting everything I can put into it from my workshop so that you can work my program for yourself without my help. Not everyone can come to Los Angeles for eight weeks to take my class. My current business model doesn't work for a national or international seminar business. My book is an opportunity for me to reach a zillion people and make a zillion bucks without having to show up a zillion hours a day to get it. Bingo—Zillionaire! That's what I want.

Every time I examine my business and whether or not to expand, I filter everything through my goal within the goal: I want to be small and happy and rich. I want a life full of fun, hobbies, family, and friends every day that I'm alive. I want to have dinner with my buddies. I want to play poker. I want to go to the movies with my eighty-five-year-old dad. I want to help plan the baby shower for my niece. I want to be happy every day. I want a business that I run, not one that runs me. I want work that gets me *to* a life, not work that *is* my life.

$200,000-300,000 a year sounds just ducky to me. If that sounds good to you, you're in luck—this is the book for that.

Strategy 3 | Send Out Ships to Bring Home the Zillions

"Twenty years from now, you will be more disappointed by the things you didn't do than by the ones you did do. So throw off the bow lines. Sail away from safe harbor. Catch the wind in your sails. Explore. Dream. Discover."
—Mark Twain

You can't just *wish* for money—you have to *do something* to make money. Thinking positive is great, but chanting, "Ohmmmm, I'm-making-lots-of-money-ohmmmm…" isn't going to put money in your bank account. Setting goals is great, but it's *getting* goals that counts. And gets you money to count. At the Church of Religious Science, they say, "Treat—and move your feet." Or pray, but row to shore. Instead of telling people to take action steps to achieve their goals, I say to "send out ships."

Lloyds of London is a 1936 film starring Tyrone Power and Freddie Bartholomew and is the story of the merchants in London in the nineteenth century, who built grand, tall-masted sailing ships. They would spend many months, sometimes years, building them. Then, whenever a ship was finally finished, the merchants would hire a crew, and provision the ships for the long sea voyage. It was an exciting day when the ship would weigh anchor, hoist her sails, and sail out of London harbor, on her way to trade for precious cargo—gold, jewels, silks, and spices—in the East Indies and other foreign ports. The trip would take many months, often years.

There were no communications lines open in those days: no ship-to-shore radio, no telegraph, no Internet, no cell phones. Once the ship had sailed, the merchant could do nothing more but wait and hope for that future day when the ship would return, sailing into London harbor laden with treasure. On that day, the young messenger boys like Freddie Bartholomew played in the film would run from the docks to the merchant's offices, shouting the news, "Your ship has come in!" And that's where the expression "waiting for my ship to come in" comes from.

You can't wait for your ship to come in if you haven't sent any out!

But you can't wait for your ship to come in if you haven't sent any out! If you haven't built ships, hired crews, and launched them, waiting for your ship is going to be a very long wait. And you will probably starve to death at the dock while you're waiting. Then you'll be moaning, "Why does this always happen to me? Everyone else's ships come in but mine. Why don't I ever have any ships come in? That's the story of my life."

Sound familiar? Do you know anyone who talks like that? If you expect your fortune to come sailing in on the next tide, you had better get busy and send out some ships. Build ships! Hire crews! Chart the route! Lift the sails! Go sailing!

Are You a Merchant, Crew, or Passenger?

If you work for yourself, are an independent contractor, or own a small business, you are the merchant who builds the ships. If you are employed working in someone else's business or are the stay-at-home spouse who contributes support to the worker in the family, you are their crew. If you aren't working or paying your way in some fashion, you are a passenger—perhaps even a stowaway. Pirates are those who steal other people's ships. You need to honestly determine which of these you are, and which are the people around you. If you figure out who's who in your relationships—at home and at work—you will avoid a lot of frustration, hurt, anger, and poverty.

Every Merchant Needs a Crew

Several years ago, I was helping a young couple figure out their financial goals. One of them was clearly a merchant. Sally was very successful in her own business, and was making most of the family income. Todd, her husband, had a business also, but he didn't get work very often. He said what he really wanted was to be an artist—but he wasn't doing much to make that happen, either. Sally wanted to help her husband become more successful so that they could move up the food chain. She was frustrated that he wasn't enthusiastic about working.

As I talked with them, it soon became apparent that their goals were very different. Her husband really didn't care about having more money, bigger houses, or better stuff. He was happy just the way things were. And if things didn't go well and they didn't have as much money, he'd happily adjust to a lower standard of living. That was fine with him. His goal was freedom and not having to work.

After listening to them both talk about their goals and desires, I turned to Sally and said, "I see the problem. You are treating him as though he were a merchant. But he's not a merchant. He is unwilling to send out any ships to make either of his goals happen. He doesn't want to work at this business he has, or even at the one he says he wishes he had. He's not crew, either, because he's not helping you with yours. He's a passenger."

Sally was depressed about that at first. She had to give up her dream that Todd would catch fire and enjoy working in a business. He wasn't a merchant like she was, and didn't want to be one. All her efforts to cajole, bribe, threaten, inspire, or otherwise motivate him to merchant status were doomed to failure.

After recovering from her disappointment, instead of trying to get him to be what he wasn't, she took a good look at what he was. Together they looked for a crew position that would suit him. What he was really good at, and loved doing, was renovating houses. So they bought a fixer house and he happily worked on improvements that increased the value of the property. He found the work he enjoyed so that it didn't feel like work. He also started helping her more often with her work. Although he didn't have the makings of a merchant, he became a tremendously supportive hard-working crew member: first mate!

Every Crew Needs a Merchant

People who are business owners or in sales understand that they are personally responsible for creating their own money. It is more difficult for employees who work for wages to see that they are, too. One evening, I spoke to a group comprised mostly of women who were employees or who didn't work outside the home. It was much more difficult for this group to see how they could have a positive effect on their income, or what sales could possibly have to do with them. This group was also skeptical of affirmations—I could see it on their faces. One woman said, "But what can I do to increase my income? I work for the state as a schoolteacher. The pay is set by the state and I can't do anything about it."

I said, "Maybe you can't do anything about the pay currently set by the state. But what else can you do? Remember, you chose to work as a schoolteacher with a set pay scale. I made a different choice. I'm a teacher too, but I am in charge of what I get paid. I set my rate and I can change it anytime I want.

"But let's say you love teaching public school but just want to improve the pay. What else can you do to make that happen?" I continued. "Perhaps you could get active in the Teachers Union, or political action groups that support merit pay for teachers. You could work for a political candidate who supports teachers. You could run for office yourself, in order to have a say in what teachers are paid. You could develop your own business during your off hours like Michelle Anton recommends in her book *The Weekend Entrepreneur*. You can change your income, but you have to take action—send out ships—to make it happen."

> **I could brainstorm a thousand ideas with someone willing to do the work to change their circumstances.**

I could brainstorm a thousand ideas with someone willing to do the work to change their circumstances. But some people just want to complain about what they don't have and can't do, rather than get creative and do whatever it takes to change it. Often the crews are jealous of the merchants. They see the merchant's ship come in and want the riches, fine houses, cars, vacations, and perks that are overflowing from the holds. On the day they see the merchant's results, they want them, too.

They have forgotten about the years of hard work and financial risks the merchant took to build that ship, and all the ships that sank before reaching the dock. A bookkeeper who once had her own business came to work in my business management firm. She was relieved at not having to network to find clients, make sales calls, or worry about collections anymore. She cheerfully waved goodbye to me every night at five o'clock, saying, "I'm so glad I'm not you!" But I remember how her face fell several years later when I bought a new Mercedes. When I asked her about her reaction, she said petulantly, "Well, I'd like to have a Mercedes, too." I reminded her what she could do to get one—spend some time outside of work going to networking meetings, making some sales calls, bringing in new clients to the business…She sighed. Nope, she didn't want to do that.

Then don't expect the same rewards as the people who do.

"Yeah, but…" Redux

Don't complain to me that my program doesn't work for you because you've chosen to put yourself in a box. If you've given away your power to make money to somebody else in a corporation or government who *you think* says you can only make this much and no more, no one is to blame but you. Instead of looking at what *doesn't* work, you need to actively search out what *will* work.

Too many people sit in their "Yeah, but" position, and just sigh and enumerate all the reasons why they can't change anything, why they can't make more money, why it's too hard, why their case is different, why it's never been done in their industry, job, profession, you name it, before, why they tried it once twelve years ago and it didn't work, yada, yada, yada.

As Werner Erhard once said, "You can have what it is you want, or you can have your reasons for not having it." That is the bottom line truth of how you create your life the way you want or justify why

If you've given away your power to make money to somebody else in a corporation or government who *you think* says you can only make this much and no more, no one is to blame but you.

it isn't the way you want. When you say, "Yeah, but," you are justifying your reasons for not changing, not taking action, not improving your life, not making money, not having fun, and generally not getting what you want. And it isn't your fault. The world just isn't fair!

Can you hear the whining in it? You practically can't say these things *without* whining. You have to stop whining if you want to start winning. Zeros whine. Zillionaires win.

Everyone's in Shipping

If you don't own your own business now, maybe you will sometime in the future. Or your spouse will, or your mom or dad will, or your best friend will. Or the merchant you go to work for will. This next section will explain what ship sending is all about, and what you will need to do if you want to operate a business. Read it even if all you want to do is sign on as crew to assist someone else to operate a business. In order to rise to the top of the crew heap, you'd better know how merchants think and what they need so you can help them manage the shipping.

To be a merchant is to own your own life. You know that you are the master of your fate, that you determine what you will do and what you won't do. You know it is your actions that build the ships, your actions that sail the ships, and your actions that bring in the ships. You won't make any money unless you provide a product or service for others. And you won't find them unless you send out scouting ships to search for them.

I own my own business teaching workshops, giving speeches, and writing books. Learning what to teach, how to give a speech, how to write—those come under the heading of building the ships. Once the ships are built, having learned my trade and honed my skills, next I have to find customers who need my services. This means sales and marketing—or sending out ships—to find my customers.

If you are in business for yourself, you had better get used to the idea that you have a sales job. Let me say it again: *you have a sales job*. You are in business to sell your product or service. If you don't do it, you will be out of business. If you aren't willing to be in sales, then go get a job working for someone who is. Because if you don't sell your product or service, there will be no money. If there is no money, there will be no business, and you will be out looking for a job.

> **If you are in business for yourself, you had better get used to the idea that you have a sales job. Let me say it again: *you have a sales job*.**

If you aren't in business for yourself, then you are crew—you have a job or you are looking for a job. A job working for somebody who owns their own business who has a sales job. Looking for a job is trying to make a sale, too, with only one difference: You are looking for just one customer instead of multiple customers. And if you get your wish and get a job, you will be selling that one customer on keeping you employed with promotions, raises, bonuses, perks, stock options, etc. every day you work there. Or you will be replaced by someone who does a better job of selling themselves than you. When you have a job, you had best pay attention to what the business sells and how to facilitate that. Employees who contribute most to the bottom line of the company are better appreciated and better paid.

We are all in sales. You might as well fall in love with this idea now, because that is all there is.

If you are the support spouse and don't work outside the home, you are crew for your spouse. That requires selling, too, or you will wake up one day divorced.

Is everybody with me now? We are all in sales. We are all in shipping. You might as well fall in love with this idea now, because that is all there is.

Big Cruise Ships and Little Canoes

I asked a friend who was in a multi-level marketing business what the truth was about networking marketing. She looked at me thoughtfully and then said, "The bottom line is this: somewhere, somehow, somebody's got to sell soap."

That's the bottom line—that's where the money is. All the money generated in any multi-level company is from the sale of a product. There are lots of people making small money sending small ships and selling a few products. The big ships and the big money in networking marketing are in enrolling other people in the business.

Then you are a sales manager: Your job is to help lots of people enroll in the business and manage them to sell lots of product. And you get a sales manager's bonus—a percentage of the business that other people in your downline produce. That is being a merchant with a fleet of ships instead of just one. As someone once told me, "I'd rather have ten percent of a watermelon than one hundred percent of a grape."

There are big ships and little ships, big sales and smaller sales. Your definition of big ships—cruise ships—will depend on your business. Big ships are large sales or multiple orders—this could be selling one hundred thousand necklaces to Bloomingdale's, getting a big advance for your book from a major publisher, selling your software company for $80 million. Medium ships— schooners—would be smaller sales like selling one thousand bracelets to Nordstrom, getting paid for a national magazine article, selling off a portion of your business for half a million dollars. Little ships—canoes—are your daily one-by-one sales. One item, one buyer, one sale equals one small ship.

The sales calls are where my money is.

In my home-based workshop business, a big ship is giving a keynote speech at a conference, being interviewed on a radio show, selling multiple copies of my book to a network marketing organization or a corporation. Anything I do that reaches many people at once is a cruise ship. A radio show is an aircraft carrier, and a national television show is a space ship. Schooners are attending local networking meetings and introducing myself to the crowd. Canoes are the phone calls I make to people I met who expressed an interest in my work. These little canoes are my sales calls—and the sales calls are where my money is. Selling happens when I have a conversation with a prospective buyer who can say, "Yes, I'd love to buy your books" or "Yes, I'd love to take your workshop."

Note: Big ships sail slower, so big sales take longer. It took me four years to write my first book, find an agent, find a publisher, and get the book in the bookstores. I couldn't stop teaching my workshops in order to write, or I'd have starved to death long before that ship came in. I depend on my canoes for my bread and butter. Likewise, you may need a full-time or part-time job while you build a business on the side. Then you can quit when your business starts producing enough profit for you to live on.

It's Not Net-sit, It's Not Net-eat—It's Net-work!

If you are a sole practitioner or have a home-based business, you are likely to get lonely sometimes. You have no office cohorts, no company cafeteria, no water-cooler or lunchroom to hang out in and chat with folks to ease a stressful day. The evil temptations arise then: Somehow the refrigerator door opens of its own accord and ice cream jumps out into your bowl as if by magic. The television or radio clicks on (by itself), and that talk show is just so interesting today, and look! It's about people in home-based businesses, too, so you convince yourself it's work-related. Or you get lost in research, i.e., surfing the web, answering and sending emails…ahhh, and where did the day go? I've been so busy!

But how come I didn't make any money?

The answer to this problem is to join a networking group. Otherwise known as "relationship marketing," networking at its best is fun, meeting good friends over a good meal and referring business to each other wherever possible. It is a support group of like-minded business people who cheer each other on to ever-greater successes. When everyone in the group is focused on finding referrals for everyone else in the group, the result is lots of business for everyone.

Networking is important to climbing the ladder of corporate success, too. You need to know who the players are in your industry, you need to make connections for your next move to the higher rung, you need to be seen by others as a mover-and-shaker.

I've been a member of one networking group for over twenty years. It's very funny when I'm at a meeting and mention this fact—someone always comes over to me, wide-eyed, and asks, "So is it working for you?" Duh.

The simple fact is networking works if you work it. You can't just go to one meeting every other month, give three people your business card, and wait for the phone to ring. If you're in business for yourself, you have to make the phone ring in other people's offices.

The simple fact is networking works if you work it. You can't just go to one meeting every other month, give three people your business card, and wait for the phone to ring. If you're in business for yourself, you have to make the phone ring in other people's offices. The best way to make a networking group work for you is to remember three simple principles: visibility, credibility, and likability.

Visibility

You've got to make a commitment of time and energy—pick a group, a regular meeting schedule, and show up consistently. Create an entertaining way of introducing yourself. People begin to develop trust in you when you are a regular attendee of a meeting. It takes some time for this to happen, so don't quit before you've given it a full year of consistent effort. When people just show up a few times and then stop coming, I refer to them as "smash and grabbers" like the burglars who smash a window, grab all they can in a few short minutes, and then disappear. I want to do business with people I'm going to see again next Tuesday.

My story: When I started networking, I owned a bookkeeping service. Everyone I met asked me what kind of work I did, and I would answer, "I'm a bookkeeper." The reactions were swift and instantaneous. People frowned, drew back, changed the subject, and left in a hurry. No one seemed anxious to have a conversation about budgets, general ledgers, and income statements. As an actress, I knew when I was losing my audience, so something had to be done— fast.

I did what I always do when I don't know how to do something: I found someone who did know, and signed up for his class. "You have to be interesting in thirty seconds or people will turn off, peg you in a category from which you will never escape," Gene Call, the instructor, said. "Never say, 'I'm a ___,' because people will lump you in the box with everyone else they ever met who did that." He suggested instead that you state it as the benefit you provide to others: "I grant people's champagne dreams and caviar wishes" (financial planner) or "I send people around the world to exotic locations" (travel agent).

That made sense to me, so I started saying, "I do financial stress reduction," and suddenly, I had people's attention. They laughed, leaned in closer, and wanted more information. One woman rolled her head back, and sighed a long, breathy, "Ahhhh…"

Reframe your own self-introduction today.

Well, I knew *she* was signing up for my class. Reframe your own self-introduction today. You're not a "computer repairman"—you are a computer magician. You're not a "mechanical engineer"—you build space ships. You're not a "therapist"—you help people navigate their ships through rough seas. You're not a businessperson—you're a money-making machine!

Credibility

Do a good job, honestly and with integrity. Be professional, always return phone calls, be on time, keep your word. If you can, join a committee, work on the board of directors, become an officer. That will increase your visibility and at the same time people will see you are a contributor to the success of the organization. (Not only am I going to see you next Tuesday, but I'm going to see you being a *leader*.) Look for the opportunity to refer business to as many other people in the group as possible. Call people and ask them what kind of clients they are looking for. What goes around comes around—if someone were referring a lot of business your way, wouldn't you be on the lookout to return the favor?

Becky's Story: Becky Bascom was working as the secretary to a mortgage broker. He was nudging her to become a broker herself, but she was terrified. She wanted to do it, but how was she going to get clients? "Network!" I told her. "Never!" she cried. Literally, she cried—big crocodile tears. She didn't feel comfortable in groups, didn't want to sell, didn't want to leave her comfort zone. But, eventually, leave it she did. I dragged her to a meeting I was attending, introduced her around, and smiled as I watched her get more and more comfortable. People were friendly and made Becky feel welcome. She opened up, started reaching out to others, and let her personality shine through her fears. It wasn't long before she joined the club and attended meetings on a regular basis. A year later, she was president of the chapter. During that year, she increased her income five times her original salary—just through making friends while networking.

Likability

People do business with people they like. Not everyone in every group is going to be your best friend, but you can reach out, shake someone's hand, and smile. This is your opportunity to greet old friends and meet new ones. The temptation will be strong to find a few buddies and sit with them every meeting. Don't do it! Pretend you are the hostess of the meeting and welcome the newcomer into your group. Practice your positive assertions and talk yourself up into good, friendly energy. Leave your complaints at home. Then I'll look forward to seeing you on Tuesday.

Diana's story: Diana Drake is a natural comedienne. Every time she does her round robin introduction, I laugh—even though I've heard it a thousand times by now. She always has a smile on her face, puts her hand out, and welcomes everyone she sees. I heard it said that a friend is someone whose face lights up when they see you. Her face lights up everyone, and you always feel a little better after you've talked with her. I know that sometimes she must feel badly or out-of-sorts, but you can't tell. She leaves her problems at the door and focuses on

Try helping others feel comfortable, and you'll find you feel more comfortable too. Like people and people will like you back!

you. She's the president of a networking chapter, and it is one of the most successful chapters in the organization. Not everyone has that natural charisma, but you can develop your own. Try helping others feel comfortable, and you'll find you feel more comfortable too. Like people and people will like you back!

If you remember these three principles and follow these instructions, you'll have so many new friendships, clients, and referrals, you won't remember what loneliness was like. And there's a side benefit—you'll make a lot of money, too.

So what are you doing next Tuesday?

"Are You George?" Party Networking

There are many business networking groups in every city. If you can't find one, start one. But you don't have to restrict yourself to business organizations. Parties are unofficial networking groups. One year, my friend Victoria invited me to her New Year's Day party. She introduced me to a woman who was enjoying reading my book.

"You have to meet George!" she told me. "He has your book and he has been faithfully reading it one page every day. He would love to meet you."

It's always fun to talk to a fan—so I set off in search of George. I didn't know what he looked like, and there were a lot of men at the party, so I waltzed up to the first man I saw and said, "Hi! Are you George?"

The man shook his head and said, "No, I'm not. Why are you looking for George?"

"Someone told me that he was a fan of my book and wanted to meet me," I replied.

"Oh, really? You're an author? What book did you write?" the man asked.

"It's called *The Wealthy Spirit…*" and all of a sudden I am networking and telling this man all about who I am and what I do.

After a pleasant conversation, exchange of contact numbers and information, I continued my search for George with the next man I saw.

"Excuse me, are you George?" I smiled sweetly.

"Nope. Who's George?…" More networking.

"I'm looking for George. Are you George?"

"No. Why are you looking for George?…"

I was getting giddy. This was the best pick-up line I'd ever used. This same conversation happened over and over. I met every man at the party before I found George. I decided that I might use it at every party I go to. You can use it, too. Invent an imaginary George, and use it as an excuse to talk to anyone you want.

Any event can turn into a networking opportunity. You can network in line at the grocery store, while pumping gas at the gas station, riding in an elevator. My networking paid off even when I was on jury duty. The judge said, "It would be nice for all of us to get to know each other. Let's go around the room and everyone say their name and what they do for a living." I was amazed—we were going to do round robin on jury duty! So when it was my turn, I said, "I'm Chellie Campbell and I treat money disorders—spending bulimia and income anorexia." There was a shout of laughter at that, and I held up my book (always prepared for book promotion, I had a copy of my book with me, of course) and said, "I'm also the author of the book *The Wealthy Spirit.*"

I sold five books.

You never know when networking is going to pay off. I've sold my book to telemarketers who called to sell me something. I bought a ring watch off the Internet, and the seller wrote me a cheerful note, so I wrote her back and suggested she might enjoy my book. She emailed me an hour later: *Chellie, I just went in and read a few of the pages on Amazon—what a great book! I'm going to buy it and I think I'll get one for my son, too—no, I know I'll get one for my son too. Thanks so much, Elaine, Glitz Galore.*

> You never know what great people might be out there unless you reach out and share a bit of yourself along the way.

Now, isn't that fun? You never know what great people might be out there unless you reach out and share a bit of yourself along the way. Why not strike up a conversation today with someone new? You may be surprised with the results.

Is It Marketing or Is It Selling?

Networking is simply meeting and having conversations with people who might be interested in you and your product or service. It is important to know that networking is *marketing*—not selling. The difference between the two is vital. It can make the difference between having a thriving business or a dying business.

The difference became clear to me when I hired a woman to help me make sales for my workshop business. She was bright, fun, and energetic, and I was very optimistic about her being able to enroll additional people for my Financial Stress Reduction workshops. But I soon found out that, although she was happily marketing me wherever she went, she was not making any sales. She was attending networking meetings and telling everyone what a great workshop I had, encouraging people to call me. She thought up great ideas for promotional giveaways, advertising displays, and attendance at conventions. This was all very nice. But those things cost me money; they didn't make me money.

After a few weeks, I asked her how many prospects she had that might enroll.

"Oh, I've talked with so many people!" she said.

"Great! But that's not what I need to know," I replied. "How many people have said 'Yes, I'm coming on this date' and paid the money?" I asked.

"Well, no one has done that," she replied.

I suggested that she make out a list of follow-up calls she could make to all the people she had talked to. Then she could project how many would say yes when she asked them to enroll. She dug her heels in at that point.

"Wait. That's not what I want to do," she said. "I don't want to have a *quota*!" She hissed the word *quota* as though I had just asked her to appear naked at the next meeting.

I explained that in order to pay her, she had to make me some money by closing some sales. After some discussion, we agreed that we saw the nature of the job differently. She wanted to do marketing. She wanted to go to lots of meetings and tell people I was wonderful, give out little gifts like chocolate wrapped like gold coins, and basically spread the word about who I was and what I did. But she didn't want to actually enroll anyone. Her activities were fun for her,

Whether you are doing the sales yourself or have someone assisting you to do it, you need to generate income, or you won't be in business for long.

but I needed more quantifiable results. I wanted her to actually enroll people and bring in money.

Since we didn't come to a meeting of the minds, we agreed to a parting of the ways.

After that experience, I made a checklist to make sure I was always conscious of what was "marketing" and what was "selling." Whether you are doing the sales yourself or have someone assisting you to do it, you need to generate income, or you won't be in business for long. Here is my checklist:

Marketing	Selling
Costs money = expense	Makes money = income
General description of product or service	Specific benefits for a particular buyer
No close, no money paid	Deal closed, money paid
Bad Paper: administrivia	Good Paper: cash, check, credit card
Letters and thank-you notes	Telephone thank you and request referrals
Networking meetings	Individual meetings and phone calls
Talking	Listening
Leaving messages	Having conversations
Undefined goals and unmeasurable results	Specific goals and measurable results
"Whenever you're ready" statement	"When will you be ready?" question
Information given: presentations	Information gotten: interview prospect

Answers
Someday

Questions
Monday, Tuesday, Wednesday,
Thursday, Friday, Saturday,
or Sunday

Marketing is important—you have to let people know you exist. That's why television commercials and ads in newspapers and magazines run over and over again. That's why networking works—you are your own commercial every time you show up. But marketing isn't enough—you still need to sell. You need to call the people you met when you were networking, so that you can have a conversation that might lead to a sale. Don't try to sell anything at the networking meeting—you'll get annoyed when somebody interrupts you, and besides, you'll find yourself locked into one conversation with one person and miss meeting the fifty other people there. If you just spend a few minutes with many people, you'll have fifty people to call the next day.

Marketing is important—you have to let people know you exist. But marketing isn't enough—you still need to sell.

A study by the Direct Marketing Association showed that sales generated through the telephone outpaced any other marketing method. In the year 2000, these were the numbers:

Newspapers $239 billion
Television $117.6 billion
Magazines $91.3 billion
Telephone $611.7 billion

And you've been wondering why there are so many telemarketers...

The Money Is in the Phone

Some people think that attending networking meetings, putting an ad in a newspaper or directory, or hanging out a business sign is enough, that you can then just sit back and wait for people to call you. If it was that easy, everybody would be doing it. Even interested parties need to be motivated to take action. It's hard to call strangers—even when you want what they have. A friend of mine told me she told two people at a networking meeting that she wanted to buy services from them, and to call her the next day. Can you believe they didn't call her? Why are they bothering to network? As Abraham Lincoln said, "Things may come to those who wait, but only the things left by those who hustle."

Many business owners are resistant to the idea of selling. They have been turned off by the old-school model of pushy salespeople. You know the one I mean—selling refrigerators to Eskimos, the model that told us that the real selling began when the customer said "no." The idea was that good salespeople overcame all objections and practically forced people to buy, regardless of whether or not they wanted and needed the product. As motivational speaker Dave Grant once told me, "That's just zapping people." The problem is, once you've zapped somebody once, they run when they see you coming. Then you have to work hard forever, because you have to find new people to zap. There's no repeat business for zappers.

Most people hate zappers. And many hate the idea of being a zapper themselves even more. So they avoid calling people because they don't want to bother anybody, instead of learning how to do it properly. These people are usually struggling financially.

The problem with telemarketers is that they sound like zappers. They don't give a hoot about you—and it shows. They are calling a zillion people a day and reading a script. And it *sounds* like they are reading a script. When they call me, I know they don't know me and they don't care about me. They just want to sell me their stuff. Every now and then I get a good one who sounds like a human being and relates to me as a person. Then I might listen to their pitch.

It's Not Cold Calling—It's Gold Calling!

Cold calling sounds like what it is—harsh and cold. But since the money is in the phone, I call it "Gold Calling." My telephone is spray painted gold and I wear gold fingernail polish to remind me to dial the golden phone. All the money you want is waiting for you at the other end of the phone. But you have to pick it up and reach out and touch someone. Selling isn't about zapping. It isn't about you. Selling is serving. You are searching for the people who need and want what you have—who are praying for you to show up with it—and helping them to have it.

> **Since the money is in the phone, I call it "Gold Calling."**

Cold calling works. But the percentage of ships that come in is very small in relation to the number you have to send out, unless you are very good at finding your target market. I know an accountant who has a lot of clients in the restaurant business. She cold calls restaurants every Tuesday and introduces herself to see if they need her services. She doesn't always enjoy it that much, but it works, so she does it.

I prefer to network. Then all of my calls are warm calls. I've met these people already and we have a mutual interest in each other. This is a much easier phone call to make than a cold call to someone you don't know.

Even if you don't have your own business, calling skills are important—perhaps you want to raise funds for your favorite charity, help your Scout troop sell cookies, or set up interviews with companies for your next job. But if you don't have your own business, why not? It could be a terrific source of additional income eventually, even if it's just a hobby on the side for now. You can meet a lot of new people and develop your financial and social skills at the same time.

> **Even if you don't have your own business, calling skills are important.**

It can be a tax write-off, a source of additional income during retirement, or it just might end up being the most fun and profitable thing you ever did for yourself. Take a risk and try it. There are many valuable multi-level marketing companies that will train you while you learn to earn.

I have found making sales calls—sending out ships—is the single most important action missing from most people's game plan. In networking groups everywhere, I meet chiropractors, acupuncturists, attorneys, massage therapists, escrow officers, real estate professionals, mortgage brokers, computer technicians, bookkeepers, interior designers, architects, cosmetologists, hair stylists, beauty consultants, writers, musicians, artists, actors, accountants, insurance brokers, financial planners, personal and business coaches, website designers, travel agents, florists, etc. They are at networking meetings in order to get business. They are happy to go to the meetings and say hello to people, but most never pick up the phone and call the people they meet. They think the idea is to give everyone their business card. They have the illusion that if people are interested, they will call.

Let me give you a tip: they aren't going to call you. Why? Because they have a life, they have priorities, they need clients themselves, they have another appointment, it's their mother's birthday, they have to wash their hair. You and what you have to offer are way down at the bottom of their priority list. Even if what you have is what they most need and close to the top of their list, they aren't going to call you. They have fears. They have objections: you're going to charge too much, they really should remodel their house first, maybe you aren't really the best one for the project, it's too far to drive, they'd have to convince their significant other and that might mean an argument and that would lead to problems and oh it's just easier to forget the whole thing...

Let me give you a tip: they aren't going to call you.

Not to mention that calling strangers on the phone is scary. You don't know how you are going to be received, or if someone is going to be nice to you, or if they are somehow going to manipulate you into buying something you don't need and spending more than you can afford to spend. You're afraid you might be calling a con artist who is going to promise you the world and rob you blind. And what if they're angry and mean to you if you say no? What people want most in the world is love and acceptance and the biggest risk when you call a stranger is that you not only won't be loved, but you'll get screamed at.

So you can see how most people find it much easier to just wait and dream that their phone is ringing off the hook with people calling to give them money...

Then there are all the people who do pick up the phone and make the sales call, but who do it badly. They call and immediately start talking about themselves: "Hi, this is Charlie. Let me tell you about me!" That's an immediate turn-off. And right then, when their prospect is turned off, they launch into a long presentation about their stuff, not even knowing if it is anything you need or want. How would they know after meeting you for two minutes? You instinctively know this person is focused on their own needs and problems and not on serving you. How's your trust level then?

Don't try to sell people your product or service bang out of the gate. Try to get to know someone. Ask about their business. Wait until they ask you before talking about your product or service. Then they are a willing listener and you have an opening to interest them in what you have to offer. No, don't wait an hour for them to get around to you—if it's taking that long, you've probably called someone who has too much time on their hands or is trying to avoid making sales calls. Have an exit line ready for those occasions, like, "Oh, I can see that I could talk to you all day, but my next appointment has just arrived," or "I'm so sorry but I have to wash my hair now…" (just kidding).

But no business is going to get transacted after a networking meeting unless *someone* makes a phone call. Somebody has to go first. And since you're reading this, that somebody is you.

Double Your Income by Tracking Your Shipping on Ship's Logs

When someone says yes and pays me money to do my work, that's my ship coming in. When someone says "no," that's a ship lost at sea. I track all the shipping—yeses and nos—on a "Ship's Log."

I didn't always track the ships. Yeah, and I didn't always make a lot of money, either. I was fuzzy about the concept of sales. Now sales are in sharp focus in the forefront of my mind and my business.

You had better get used to sending out lots of ships, because not all of your ships make it back to home port. Perhaps the one you're waiting for just ran aground outside of the harbor. Or sank in the hurricane a week after leaving the dock. Or got commandeered by pirates, or lost in the whirlpool. Remember the mutiny on the *Bounty*? That ship sat at Pitcairn Island for twenty years. And does the name *Titanic* mean anything to you?

Like the London merchants, once you send the ship out, it's out of your control. You are only in charge of sending it out, not when it comes in. It's all about percentages. You have to send out many ships in order to insure that at least some of them make it back to port with treasure enough to feed you. And most of the bigger ships need at least two tugboats.

If you master the art of sending out ships, and then count the number of ships sent versus the number of ships that come in, you will have the exact formula for doubling your income. Or tripling it. Or multiplying it by whatever number you want. If you have to send out ten ships in order to have one ship come in, you have to send out twenty ships if you want two ships to come in. If it takes twenty ships to have one ship come in, you have to send out forty ships in order to get two. It's the simplest math there is. And more people fail this math test than any other I know of.

> **If you master the art of sending out ships, and then count the number of ships sent versus the number of ships that come in, you will have the exact formula for doubling your income.**

Why? Because they don't count their ships. People like to stay vague about what they are doing to produce their income, so they can think they are doing more than they are doing. Then they don't have to do the scary stuff like selling. And they can moan and complain that they're not making any money but it's not their *fault!* Life just isn't fair!

Yes, it is. If you need twenty clients a week to make the income you want and you only have seven, how many ships do you have to send out? I can't tell you how many people answer, "Three." Please tell me, how is sending out three ships going to equal thirteen more clients every week? It's going to be a long wait at your dock.

SHIP'S LOG DESIGN

Date #	Phone Dials	# Conversations	# Set Appointments	# Meetings	# Clients
	Target/Actual	Target/Actual	Target/Actual	Target/Actual	Target/Actual
Mon.	____|____	____|____	____|____	____|____	____|____
Tues.	____|____	____|____	____|____	____|____	____|____
Wed.	____|____	____|____	____|____	____|____	____|____
Thurs.	____|____	____|____	____|____	____|____	____|____
Friday	____|____	____|____	____|____	____|____	____|____
Total	____|____	____|____	____|____	____|____	____|____

Count your ships and you will know how you create your money.

Each Monday, or the beginning of your work week, set your targets for each category: the number of times you will dial the phone, the number of conversations you will have, the number of appointments you will set with people to meet them later, the number of meetings you have scheduled for each day (networking meetings or individual appointments that were set previously), and the number of clients you expect to result from all your sales activity.

Using this form worked wonders for me. It kept me focused on what I needed to do to make my business profitable: I had to have enough conversations with people that resulted in enough sales to make a profit, pay my bills, buy some goodies, and fund my retirement account. It's no good having a workshop business and showing up to teach it when no one shows up to take it. No enrollments equals no money equals I'm out of business. I had a nightmare one night that I didn't make enough money to stay in business and had to go back to work as a secretary. For my attorney. Now I love Barbara, but I don't want to be her secretary. All I ever have to do to get myself out of my complacency and off to a networking meeting is remember that.

Then I pick up the Golden Phone—the one with the money in it—and make some calls.

When you get into the habit of sending out ships, even if you know some ships aren't going to make it back home, you can still be confident and optimistic because you know you have a whole fleet sailing out there on the ocean. This creates a positive expectation that ships are going to be sailing in, docking at your pier, and unloading riches for you any minute. Positive energy shines from you. You feel good about yourself because you've been doing what it takes to succeed. You live in the happy expectation of hearing

> **When you get into the habit of sending out ships, even if you know some ships aren't going to make it back home, you can still be confident and optimistic because you know you have a whole fleet sailing out there on the ocean.**

"Your ship has come in!" at any moment.

Remember to focus on what you want, not what you don't want. Don't send out any ships while you're dooming and glooming—those ships will sink. And when the ships do come in, celebrate! Don't just celebrate the aircraft carriers and the Queen Marys—celebrate every little canoe and kayak. Celebrate every little bit of money, gold, treasure, gifts, and compliments they bring. Appreciate all the inflow. If you have to wait for the big ship to come in before you can be happy, you'll be waiting too long. Too much life will pass you by on the dock while you're waiting, anxiously, breathlessly, hopefully, instead of living in the joyful moment of now.

You have a dream. You have a business. You have a telephone. Send out your ships!

Strategy 4 | Surround Yourself with People Who Make You Rich and Happy

"A friend is someone who knows the song in your heart and can sing it back to you when you have forgotten the words."
—Donna Roberts

I divide the world into two groups: My People and Not My People. My People are Dolphins—happy, friendly, and rich. Not My People come in two species: Sharks who want to eat you, or Tuna who want to complain to you. You can tell who's who by the way you feel after you've been with them, and the state of your bank account. Dolphins put money in your pocket and a song in your heart. Sharks rob you and leave you bleeding. Tuna cry for you but can't help you. If you want to be wealthy, you have to learn to be a Dolphin and choose your friends and co-workers wisely. Don't borrow from a loan shark. Don't ask unsuccessful people for career advice. Get Zillionaire advice from Dolphins, and you'll become one yourself.

This is how to tell which sea creatures you've been swimming with:

Dolphins: You feel good and you are rich.

Sharks: You feel bad and you are broke.

Tuna: You feel tired but you broke even.

I could make other distinctions, categorizing some people as Octopuses, Sea Horses, Barracuda, Eels, Angel Fish, etc., but having too many choices tends to confuse people. That's why I like to stick to three categories, or three points, or three rules to remember, or a menu of three choices. You can remember Low, Medium, and High Budgets and you can remember Dolphins, Sharks, and Tuna. That's all you really need to make decisions about people. Either they support you or they cost you.

Sharks sneer at books like this one. Why would anyone need a book to tell them how to be successful? Kill or be killed is all you need to know—it's survival of the fittest, dummy. Tuna don't read books except as a vehicle to beat themselves up with and cry, "Oh, no, this doesn't work for me, either. Nothing ever works for me." Dolphins value learning and growing; they read books, take workshops, attend classes, listen to CDs, and are always improving themselves and the world around them.

> **When you learn to surround yourself with Dolphins and avoid Shark and Tuna, you will be richer and happier, and so will your friends.**

When you learn to surround yourself with Dolphins and avoid Shark and Tuna, you will be richer and happier, and so will your friends. You'll be a Zillionaire among Zillionaires.

Dolphins

Dolphins are friendly creatures; they swim in groups called pods. They are intelligent and communicate with each other. They are playful, jumping for the joy of it in graceful arcs above the waves.

They have been known to ward off Shark attacks and protect other fish in the sea. There are many accounts of dolphins rescuing human beings.

People who are Dolphins are generous. They love to share the wealth and always make sure there is enough money left on the bargaining table so that everyone feels they've made a good deal. They'd like nothing better than for everyone in the world to be rich, but they understand that you have to work for it. Because of this, they are wonderful mentors and teachers and are delighted to share their secrets of success with you. They give you honest feedback, but only when requested. When you swim in the company of Dolphins, you feel empowered, energized, and uplifted. You feel better about yourself and the world around you, and you have more money, too. You will always find Dolphins swimming alongside your golden treasure ships.

Dolphins praise you and pay you.

Dolphins play Win-Win.

Swimming with Dolphins

My agent, Lisa Hagan, is a great example of a Dolphin. She took me on as a client after I sent her my book proposal for *The Wealthy Spirit*. She called me first thing the morning after she received it and said, "I'm on page twelve and I would love to represent you." We talked and giggled and recognized each other's Dolphinhood. She faxed me a contract; I signed it and faxed it back that same day.

But her true Dolphin spirit showed up over the next year and a half as we got turned down by publisher after publisher. She never lost faith in me or my book. She practiced positive thinking herself and passed my affirmations along to her employees, business associates, friends, and family. She saw the value of my work, and worked to convince publishers of that value tirelessly, just on the speculation that it would find a home and be published.

We emailed each other every week—sometimes every day. She wrote me things like this: "I think you are going to be a *huge* bestseller. They will be begging you to come to the book expo. I can't wait to be standing next to you and saying, 'Yes, she's my favorite client! She's a *star*!'" (Dolphins tend to write with lots of exclamation points. Sharks hate that.) I printed her email and pinned it up on the wall by my computer in January 1999.

It's still there.

Dolphins are not always so self-evident. Some people might think that Simon Cowell, the acerbic judge on the television show *American Idol*, is a Shark because he gives such pointed, withering criticisms to some of the singer-contestants. I consider him a Dolphin. Dolphins aren't all sweetness and light. Dolphins can be tough, but they do it for your own good. I wince over some of his criticisms when they seem particularly harsh, but the contestants take that risk when they sign up to participate in the show. If they are bad singers, they should know better, but if they didn't before, they will now. If they are good singers making mistakes, they will learn from him and improve. Besides, Simon's tough personality and witty remarks are part of why the show has been such a success. He knows that, and gives the audience—and his fellow investors, backers, producers, and the television station—what they want. It's working for everyone on whatever level they're playing the game.

Who are the Dolphins in your life? Who are your mentors and supporters?

Who are the Dolphins in your life? Who are your mentors and supporters? Who can you count on for an uplifting word of encouragement, good advice, or a safe haven from the storms that batter your ships? Who do you trust completely, unquestioningly, to hold your highest good in their heart? Who can you trust to tell you the truth when you need to hear it? Who are the clients, bosses, or partners that praise you and pay you? Whose email did you print out and post on your wall?

These are Your People. These are your Dolphins. Listen. Underneath the noise and squawk of a billion people, Dolphins are singing. Find them and swim with them.

Sharks

Sharks are eating machines. That is their sole purpose in life—eating. It's not their fault—they were born like that. They are big and have big teeth—the better to eat you with, my dear. They are on the hunt. The *Jaws* theme song plays and then they pounce. The world is their oyster—literally. They see everyone else in the world as dinner. That includes you.

Sharks are sometimes rich, but don't enjoy their wealth because the word *enough* doesn't exist in their vocabulary. Sharks don't share with anybody, because their constant thought is *Me, me, me, I, I, I* so there is no room at the dinner table for anyone else except on a plate. You will see Sharks swimming alongside pirate ships and black plague ships.

There are two kinds of Sharks: Angry Sharks and Con-Artist Sharks.

1. Angry Sharks. They are completely self-obsessed. They have no empathy for other people—they can't tell that you have thoughts and feelings just like they do. You are food. They are angry with life and the world and are going to take it out on you. These sharks tend to scream and yell and throw tantrums in order to get their way. They will tell you everything that's wrong with you if you give them an opportunity—like if you say, "Hello." Powered by rage, they are fearsome to behold. They rip you apart right away.

2. *Con-Artist Sharks*. They are Sharks in Dolphin's Clothing. They pretend to be your friend and imitate Dolphin behavior in order to get close to you. They have charisma, a hail-fellow-well-met bonhomie, and a ready smile—there's no such thing as an obnoxious con artist. But look in their eyes—you'll see nothing but calculation. They are running numbers, figuring what you are worth and how they can take advantage of you. Their offers sound so fabulous! You suspect maybe they're too good to be true, but what if it really is your lucky day at last and this is a fabulous opportunity for you to get rich? So you throw your skepticism into Davy Jones' Locker and board their Pirate Ship to search for the treasure. But you're the treasure and now they've got you walking the plank into their jaws. They are your best buddies—until they slowly rip you apart.

After you've been swimming in Shark-infested waters, you feel hurt, wounded, and betrayed. And usually, you are broke, too.

Sharks could pay you—but they don't want to. They want all the money for themselves.

Sharks play Win-Lose.

Swimming with Sharks

"Hi! Welcome to our networking group," I said to the guest, a tall gentleman in a business suit who had introduced himself as a financial planner. "I'm glad you could join us this morning."

"Thank you," he replied with a smile.

He should have stopped there. Instead, he said, "I'm glad they had a breakfast to attend instead of those dinners—they are way too expensive!"

That was the first warning sign. I was thinking to myself, Wow, he's a financial planner and he thinks the dinner is too expensive? I said, "Well, yes, the dinners aren't cheap, but it doesn't matter—think of all the business leads you will get. That more than makes up for the price of the dinner…"

He was shaking his head before I finished speaking. He wasn't having any of it.

"They're marking up the price of the dinner so much they must be making a fortune. I don't want to be contributing to the profit of the organization!"

Okay, let's add this up. He's either worried about money (Tuna) or doesn't want to spend any (Shark), and he doesn't want anyone else to make a profit from his payment (Shark). This man was off my referral list in a heartbeat. I want to work with people who are happy to pay premium prices for good value, and happy that other people are making a good living around him.

Some of you may read this story and think, What a great money manager! He's careful with his money and I'd like someone like that working with me. But swim with him at your own risk. He has a belief that money is scarce, there isn't enough to go around, and You'd Better Look Out For Number One. This man's attitude told me that, if we did business together, he would be looking out for himself first above all, and me second—if at all. That doesn't make me feel comfortable about giving him my money to manage—how about you?

Wouldn't you like your clients to pay you happily, with praise for a job well-done, rather than pay you grudgingly or complain that it cost too much or wasn't good enough? Then do the same in your own life. Pay for every product or service with joy and praise—or don't buy it. Pay the light bill with appreciation for Thomas Edison and the electric company that keeps your lights and computer working. Pay for gasoline with gratitude that there are people in the world whose job it is to make available the stuff that makes your car go. Bless every dollar out as much as you bless every dollar in. The money goes out anyway—why not send it out joyfully instead of resentfully?

Dolphins are fond of tithing, donating to charity, and contributing to those in need. That is great. But they also know that every dollar you spend is a blessing to someone and a contribution to people who are working, providing some product or service to make your life better and easier. Buy a piece of jewelry or a painting or a hand-knit scarf at a crafts fair and see how the seller lights up. They are just as happy to make a sale as you are. It's a contribution! Yes, keep within your budget, but then enjoy every dollar you spend. You will increase the flow of money into your own life when you do.

Sharks don't want any part of that giving/sharing business. That's for suckers. Sharks want to rip you off. I once knew a businessman who never felt a negotiation had gone well unless the other party was hurting. You know you've been with a Shark when your bank account is empty and you are in pain.

Tuna

Tuna are food for the Sharks. They are the Victims of the Universe, and they wear their martyr crowns and title sashes proudly. They talk endlessly about how awful life is and how badly they've been treated and how it isn't their fault. It's a one-way conversation—all they want from you is a sympathetic "oh, poor thing!" now and then.

Tuna complain a lot and don't accomplish much. They would love to share, but they can't because they're broke, and could you please invest in their business or loan them some money so they can save the world through their non-profit organization? You will find Tuna swimming alongside fishing boats, looking for a handout. They get hauled in instead, and handed out to someone else. They don't get dinner—they *are* dinner.

Tuna come in two species: Angry Tuna and Timid Tuna.

1. Angry Tuna. They are the "Ain't It Awful" or "Doesn't It Suck" people who complain endlessly about everything. They never *do* anything about anything, mind you, they just whine and complain. "Life is Unfair" and "What's the Use" are their mottos. Angry Tuna will hurt you almost as badly as a Shark will, but they will do it through passive-aggressive behavior. Their inaction will cost you a contract, cost you a friendship, cost you a fortune. And they will get huffy if you say anything to them about it, because They Are Blameless. Nothing is ever their fault.

2. Timid Tuna. They never do anything, either, because they are afraid. They mask their ineffectual behavior under the guise of being Self-Sacrificing and Good-Hearted, but really they are just Victims. They justify playing with Sharks, saying, "Oh, there's really a Dolphin in there somewhere—I'm going to help them find their inner Dolphin," meanwhile completely oblivious to the fact that they're missing a fin and the blood in the water is their own. Timid Tuna won't cause you direct harm, but they will make you really, *really* frustrated.

Both kinds of Tuna end up as dinner. And you'll be in the frying pan with them, salted and breaded, if you swim with them very often. After you've spent some time with Tuna, you feel tired and depressed and need to take a nap. It's hard to get anything done after that.

Tuna can't pay you. Tuna have no money.

Angry Tuna play Lose-Lose. Timid Tuna play Lose-Win.

Swimming with Tuna

I received an email from "Christine" titled "Single mom needs help." I get a lot of email from people interested in my work, so I opened it. It said: "I am desperately in need of financial and legal help. I don't have time to explain. Please call 404-xxx-xxxx so we can talk."

I closed the email and promptly deleted it.

This is either a spam-scam from a Shark or a panic attack from a Tuna. I'm not going to waste my time or energy on either. Don't have time to explain your situation? Then why should I spend my time and my money making a long distance call to you? If this came from a Shark, this is someone preying on the potential good nature of the email recipient to want to help others. Who knows where the phone call could take you? Perhaps this is a number that charges you a fee per minute.

> **There is help all around you in this world, but you have to develop the contacts and the community of people who could and should care about you.**

If this is from a Tuna, it really is someone in trouble. But why are they reaching out to me—someone they don't know? My name and/or book, workshops, or website weren't mentioned. Why did they contact me and not government agencies, social services, family, friends, business associates, neighbors, their church, temple, or synagogue, any local charity, etc.? There is help all around you in this world, but you have to develop the contacts and the community of people who could and should care about you. You have to take care of your relationships with people. Then you don't have to reach out in desperation to a complete stranger thousands of miles away and hope they take pity on you.

But then, Tuna tend to wear out their friends eventually. Maybe Christine had used up all her Dolphin friends. Tuna tend to call you endlessly asking for advice but never follow any of it. Then they need the same advice next week. It's all a sham. They aren't interested in your advice—they just want to cry on your shoulder and hear "oh, poor thing."

Perhaps I sound like I don't have any sympathy. I do. I'm just clear that my having compassion and pity for you won't get you anywhere. I won't wallow in weepiness with you. I want to get you up out of the doldrums and whatever thinking and behavior got you there. I want to motivate, inspire, and teach you how to get better, richer, happier. Life is great and you can have what you want!

But you won't get a great life by crying over not having one. That's a plea for negative attention, and I risk my own health and wealth if I swim with you too long.

The Craving for Attention

People crave attention so badly that even negative attention is better than no attention at all. In *The Hidden Messages in Water*, author Masaru Emoto used high-speed photography to discover that the character of crystals that formed in frozen water changed when specific thoughts were focused on them. Water that was exposed to loving words like "thank you" and "I love you" showed beautiful, complex, snowflake-like patterns and lovely colors. Water exposed to negative thoughts like "you fool" produced deformed, asymmetrical designs with dingy colors. Since the human body is about 90 percent water, we can infer that we might be affected by the thoughts others direct toward us. "Sticks and stones can break my bones, but words can never hurt me" goes the old nursery rhyme, but it's wrong. Words hurt.

One of the stories in the book that interested me most was an experiment a family tried with jars of rice. They prepared two jars, and every day for a month, they said "thank you" to one jar and "you fool" to the other jar. By the end of the month, the rice in the jar that had been told "thank you" had fermented, with a mellow malt-like smell. The rice in the other jar had rotted and turned black.

Another family decided to try the experiment for themselves, but they prepared a third jar of rice along with the other two. This jar they simply ignored. What do you think happened to the rice in the third jar? It actually rotted more quickly than the rice that had been told "you fool." Dr. Emoto said that others tried this same experiment with the same results. He wrote that "it seems that being ridiculed is actually not as damaging as being ignored…The most damaging form of behavior is withholding your attention."

People need attention to thrive and grow. Any attention is better than none.

People who feel ineffectual have a tendency to blame and complain because they are starved for attention. They are willing to suffer many things in order to be noticed and get acknowledgement, even if it's negative. They become Sharks or Tuna. Children act out in destructive ways, begging for parental boundaries. Some people who don't have the patience to develop talents and abilities as Dolphins get the attention by screaming and destroying. People need attention to thrive and grow. Any attention is better than none.

How to Get Rid of Sharks

1. Don't Be a Sucker, e.g., Tuna

As P.T. Barnum said, "There's a sucker born every minute." Suckers are Tuna, and your job is to not be one. Don't answer the emails from Africa that come from someone purporting to be the wife of some deceased official who needs you to loan her the use of your bank account and you'll be paid millions of dollars. Please. Does it make any sense that out of all the people in the world, they don't know anyone else but you? No, and you didn't win the ten-million-dollar sweepstakes you didn't enter, either. Surprise.

> **Suckers are Tuna, and your job is to not be one.**

Professional poker players call bad players "fish." I've seen Angry Sharks berating the fish at the poker table for playing badly. That's unkind, and it's also dumb. Experienced players know better than to make someone who is losing feel badly about playing with you. They want you to stay and continue to play badly—that's how they make money. When he sees a player criticize another player, professional poker expert and co-host of *Celebrity Poker Showdown* Phil Gordon admonishes, "Shhh. Don't tap on the aquarium." If you look around the table and you don't see who the fish is, it's you. Get out of the water.

2. Stand Up for Yourself

If you have a boss, and he or she is a Shark, let them know you aren't going to put up with any Sharky shenanigans. Draw the line in the sand at the seashore—and show it to them.

> If you have a boss, and he or she is a Shark, let them know you aren't going to put up with any Sharky shenanigans.

When I was in my Tuna phase and studying for my Dolphin credentials, I worked for Edgar Scherick, a motion-picture producer who had a reputation for yelling. I could handle it if it wasn't directed at me, but I held my breath anxiously. When he finally did scream at me one day, I fled to the bathroom, crying. I knew I couldn't stay in this job if that was going to happen again. So, heart in my throat, I walked into his office and shut the door.

"Edgar," I said, "I respectfully request that you please not yell at me again. I just had to go cry in the bathroom for a half hour, and this isn't effective time management for you or for me."

Poor dear, he looked completely taken aback. I don't think anyone had ever asked him not to yell at them.

"Oh, you shouldn't mind that, Chellie," he said. "I like you. I think you do a good job. The yelling doesn't mean anything."

"It means something to me," I said. "It's very upsetting and makes me cry. So I'd appreciate it very much if you didn't do it again."

"All right, all right," he muttered, ruffling some papers on his desk.

About three weeks later, he yelled at me again. I cried in the bathroom again. Then I walked into his office and started to close the door. Before the door shut, he started apologizing.

About four months after that, he yelled at me one more time. I yelled back at him. He never yelled at me again. Dolphin-in-training program completed.

If you're doing a good job, it's likely you won't get fired for standing up for yourself in the face of bad boss behavior. In fact, you'll get more respect from everyone and probably get promoted. But if you should get fired, celebrate it as a success. There are plenty of jobs and plenty of better bosses. If they don't change, but don't fire you, quit. You don't have to be abused, and if you sign on for that, you are dooming yourself to life in a can of Tuna.

3. Raise Their Prices

If you're employed, demand a raise. If you are self-employed and have Sharky clients, raise their prices. This is a sure-fire technique to get rid of Sharks, because an integral part of being a Shark is that they don't like to pay for anything. If they do have to pay, they want rock bottom discounts and lots of extra benefits and overtime put in by you for no extra charge. Sound like anyone you know? They're a pain in the fin.

When I had my bookkeeping service, I had a bad feeling about a new client. It was just an intuition. I didn't like some of the Sharky things they said, but nothing concrete occurred until one day when they fired a couple of employees. We were instructed to issue their final paychecks, which we did. Then the client stopped payment on their paychecks the very next day. When I found out about it, I didn't hesitate. I called the client immediately.

"Hi," I said pleasantly. "I've been reviewing your account and I see that we were just a little off in thinking how much time and attention it would take to manage your bookkeeping. We had estimated a fee of three hundred dollars per month would cover everything, but I see that it is really going to take twice as long, so we have to raise your price to six hundred dollars per month. So sorry."

"That will never do!" the man sputtered angrily. "We will find ourselves another bookkeeping service!"

I'm sure they were hoping I was a Tuna and would say, "Oh no, please don't leave. I'll do anything to keep you as a client!" When you're broke, you say things like that. But Chellie is a Dolphin now.

"I understand," I said sweetly. "We'll make arrangements for you to pick up your things."

Shark in the Family

But what do you do when the Shark in your life is in your family? This is a big "yeah, but" for a lot of people, like they were chained to these people at birth and there's nothing they can do about it. Ha.

Talk about what you agree on, and avoid topics of disagreement. Keep your conversations with them short, light, and about safe topics like the weather. Don't tell them any of your problems, and don't tell them any of your plans.

You keep people in your life by choice. You can simply sever all ties, move away, change your phone number, etc. If they are particularly toxic or abusive, this is probably an excellent idea. One client of mine shared that his wife had voluntarily arranged to put herself in a foster home at the age of fourteen in order to escape her abusive family. What courage that wee Dolphin must have had. If she can do it, you can do it.

But if you love them and want them in your life, but just wish to change some of the hurtful interactions between you, you can change the conversation. Talk about what you agree on, and avoid topics of disagreement. Keep your conversations with them short, light, and about safe topics like the weather. Don't tell them any of your problems, and don't tell them any of your plans. They will blame you for the problems and say you have no chance of getting any of your plans to work. Do you want to hear that? No, so don't give them the chance. If they ask, just say something generic like, "Everything is going well." That gives them no ammunition at all.

If you find yourself running out of steam and about to confess a failing or, God forbid, ask for advice, get off the phone or leave the party. Memorize some exit lines like, "Oh, my doorbell just rang" or "Oops, I almost forgot—I'm late for an appointment and I have to run" or the tried-and-true standby "I have to wash my hair now." Lying is not generally Dolphin behavior, but Tuna-in-recovery have my permission to lie to escape a Shark attack. When you graduate to Dolphin status, you can kindly and gently tell them the truth—that you don't appreciate their disempowering comments, and if they keep it up, you won't be talking to them anymore.

If you stand up for yourself, and you value yourself enough not to put up with bad behavior, Sharks will swim away fast. They are looking for easy pickings, not people who see through their Dolphin mask to the Shark teeth within. Good Dolphins never have any Sharks swimming around them.

Dolphin-in-Training Manual for Sharks

Sharks very rarely have any interest in becoming Dolphins. That's why after Sharks get out of prison, they do something Sharky again and go right back. I would be surprised if there are many Sharks reading this book. But just in case there is one, this is for you. If you have found that eating others isn't satisfying your inner cravings for spiritual sustenance, that you're lonely and want to improve your life, there is help for you. You can change your life if you want to. You can make a new start. Make a commitment to what you want to have in your life, choose goals, and stay on the path to getting them honestly and ethically, and you, too, can join the Dolphin pod.

Let me give you a tip: If you think you are going to use this book to save *other people* that you judge as Sharks, you are quite likely a Tuna. You know how hard it is to change yourself—and you *want* to change. You have no hope of changing someone else, except by example.

For Sharks who want to change, or Dolphins-in-training who want to control some of their Sharky urges, these are my suggestions:

1. Join a church, temple, synagogue, or other spiritual group. You need help with ethics. The best way to figure out a new ethical structure for your life is to connect with a group that is focused on spiritual values. Read spiritual books, study, meditate, and pray. Say "Thank you!" to whatever Higher Power you believe in for every good thing in your life every day. Be specific. If you can't think of anything, buy a copy of *14,000 Things to be Happy About* by Barbara Ann Kipfer and study up. Write your own gratitude journal and don't stop until you've got 14,000 things.

> **The best way to figure out a new ethical structure for your life is to connect with a group that is focused on spiritual values.**

2. Find a Dolphin to emulate. Find some Dolphins and do what they do, even if you don't understand it. Pick out a mentor at work and ask for guidance. If you have an addiction of any kind, a twelve-step program

such as Alcoholics Anonymous or any other of the Anonymous groups will provide you with many role models and a sponsor or two. Look for the people who have dried out, suit up, and show up. Follow their instructions—because they're Dolphins and you're not. In order to have what they have, you have to do what they do.

3. Work above and beyond the call of duty. Give more than you are asked to give at your job or business. Go the extra mile to help someone else. Pay more money to your employees. Give money to charity. Donate something whenever asked. Never refuse a request from your spiritual group. You've been taking a lot out of life, and now it's your turn to give.

4. Help others. Volunteer at a soup kitchen, a homeless shelter, a shelter for battered wives and their children, Meals-on-Wheels, a hospice, etc. Learn compassion for others, and then be of service to them. When they thank you with tears in their eyes, if there is hope for you, something will stir in your heart and you will change. If you can't yet relate with compassion for other people, get a dog. Volunteer at an animal shelter.

5. Watch comedies. No more cops and robbers or serial killer horror movies for you. You need to lighten up, laugh, and find joy and pleasure in funny movies and television shows. It's hard to hate when you're laughing.

Dolphin-in-Training Manual for Tuna

If you are a Tuna, there is still hope for you. You can choose to transform yourself into a Dolphin. Here's the Dolphin-in-training Program:

1. Give up blame. You will have to give up blaming other people, fate, politicians, the housing market, the economy, taxes, your

mother, your father, other family members, global warming, the Powers-That-Be, God, the CIA, the FBI, the UFOs, aliens, or anything else for what's wrong with your life. It's not them. It's you. It may have been them to begin with, but if you aren't actively sending out ships to change your situation, if you keep going back to your abuser, now it's you.

2. Give up guilt. Guilt is blame directed inward. If there's one person in the world with less money than them, Tuna feel badly about having money. Guilt doesn't improve the world. Positive action improves the world. You don't help the poor and starving by being one of them. Guilt just makes you depressed and miserable, and tends to make everyone around you depressed and miserable, too. Until they figure out you're a Tuna and swim away to play with the Dolphins.

3. Refuse to be a victim. We spend too much of our lives trying to please the unpleaseable. When I was a Tuna, I chose abusive relationships, abusive bosses, abusive clients. If there were one hundred people at a party, and ninety-nine of them liked me, I would find the one that didn't and follow them around trying to change their mind. I lived in Shark-infested waters. My fault. If you get beaten up once, it could be an accident, but if you get beaten up more than once, you signed up to be the flunky who gets in the ring with a champion boxer. Stop that. Put up with no bad behavior from anyone and you will soon find that all the people around you treat you like gold.

> **Put up with no bad behavior from anyone and you will soon find that all the people around you treat you like gold.**

4. Take 100 percent responsibility for your life. That means no more complaining. Because it's all because of you. Everything around you is a reflection of you. Your job is the one you continue to show up at, the city you live in is the one you choose to stay in, the spouse you have is the one you choose to go home to, everything in your closet is something you chose to buy or choose to keep. Maybe you didn't choose your parents to begin with (although, personally, I think you chose that, too) but you choose whether or not you keep them in your life now. You may have been born in unfortunate circumstances, but you have the opportunity to change your circumstances now.

5. Make "no" your new "yes." Tuna tend to get manipulated a lot. They have usually attracted a bunch of Sharks who are taking advantage of them and making outrageous requests. So start saying no to people. Every time you say no to someone else, you are saying yes to yourself. No you can't run the charity bake sale, no you can't pick your friend up at the airport at three o'clock in the morning, no you can't work overtime every night, no you can't baby-sit your neighbor's six kids so they can go on a two-week cruise to the Caribbean, no, no, no. After you get a lot of good nos under your belt, you can try saying yes to something. But not an immediate yes. You must say, "I'll have to check my calendar," and then take twenty-four hours to think about it first. Is it a Dolphin request or a Shark manipulation? After you have thought about it without the pressure of having to answer right away, if you want to say yes, you can. But make sure you really want to do it, and you're not just giving in to your old Tuna habits.

6. Find a Dolphin to emulate. Find a Dolphin and do what they do. Watch, listen, learn, and practice. When I left an abusive

marriage and got a job in an executive search firm, I latched on to Jennifer Martin, a recruiter in the firm. She was terrific! She was funny, fun, encouraging, uplifting, and made great money. But she had no problem telling you to take a jump off the freeway overpass when you screwed up. Whenever I said something dumb, she'd arch one eyebrow and say, "Is that right?" in a sardonic, slightly disgusted English accent. Uh oh. Whenever I heard her say that, I knew my Tuna can was leaking. I would immediately review what I had said and ask her to explain it if I didn't understand what the problem was. Dolphins aren't afraid to tell the truth. If you get hurt and swim away because of it, it's okay with them— you are then just another Tuna that didn't survive the training. Appreciate that, follow their advice, report your successes, and learn the next thing they have to teach you. As long as you are improving, Dolphins will be happy to contribute. If you wallow on the beach complaining about the heat when the cool ocean is right in front of you, you'll be left high and dry without a second thought.

Sharkometers and Tunometers Tell You Who Are the Fish in Your Sea

When meeting new people, new prospective clients, friends, bosses, or business associates, we need to make sure we eliminate Sharks and Tuna before they get close enough to eat us or leech us. We have to turn on our Sharkometers and Tunometers and listen. They will tell us who they are.

Ask a lot of questions, and listen to the answers. When they ask you about your business, watch their facial expressions and listen to their tone of voice. As an example, here are some Dolphin, Shark, and Tuna responses to the issue of pricing. The exact wording may change, but the tone of the conversation and how you feel afterward will generally be the same:

You say, "I charge _____ for my services," "My product costs _____," or "I expect _____ as a starting salary, raise, or bonus."

Dolphin Responses (often smiling and nodding) sound like this:

"That's no problem. When can we start?"

"Great!" or "It's a deal!"

"You're worth it and I want to work with you. Let's get together and talk about negotiating a deal that will work for both of us." (Dolphins have budget realities, too.)

You feel: Happy, empowered, and friendly.

What you should do next: Say, "Thank you!" Then schedule the next appointment to get together to negotiate and finalize the deal, have lunch, get to know each other better, trade referrals, and add each other to your Dolphin lists.

Angry Sharks say (rolling their eyes, sneering, or snorting):

"How do you get away with charging that?"

"You must be making a hell of a profit."

"That price is for suckers. How much of a discount are you going to give me?"

You feel: Attacked and defensive.

What you should do next: Your Sharkometer has turned bright red and is blaring warning signals. Get out of the water. Smile and say, "Yes, I am making a lot of money, thanks," and make an immediate exit. If you give them an inch, they will take your entire ocean. Even if you agreed on a reduced price, they have no intention of paying your bill. Take them off all your lists, or you'll be drowning in red ink at the end of your association.

Con-Artist Sharks (smiling and nodding like the Dolphins they pretend to be) say:

"Ah, a great price and I admire you for charging that much. But of course, we will need to make a deal on that. We'll pay you half. It'll be great business for both of us and you'll get paid more later as we grow. We have amazing plans for growing our company and we're going to be a Fortune 500 in three years and you will be a part of our team and will get so much business from your association with us and…" (They have to talk a lot to schmooze you into it, and it's always about the rich rewards you will get…later.)

You are not a non-profit organization. Resist the temptation to lower your price in order to be a good person and help the downtrodden.

You feel: Like you should feel good, but you don't. You are vaguely uneasy but can't quite put your Dolphin fin on why.

What you should do next: Your Sharkometer is quietly blinking red warning signs suggesting you may want to reach for your beach towel and dry off. This may or may not be a Shark in Dolphin's clothing. It's hard to tell, isn't it? But their not wanting to pay anywhere near your price is a good sign that you should pass on this opportunity. There are other fish in the sea.

Angry Tuna frown and sniff:

"It must be nice to be able to charge that much."

"You won't find anyone who can afford that here."

"I guess you have to charge that much to afford your nice car."

You feel: Embarrassed; like you should apologize for making money, which must mean you're not a very spiritual person.

What you should do next: Your Tunometer is hollering Code Blue. If you don't get out of the water, you're going to need a crash cart. These people think making money is bad and at the same time are jealous of you for doing it. They are poor, of course, and self-righteous about it, too. They will never tell you to your face that they think you charge too much, but they'll complain about it to 45,000 other people. If you work with them, they will criticize you every step of the way, ask for discounts, and refuse to pay for extra work because it was all your fault.

Timid Tuna smile but shrug:

"Oh, if only I had more money I would buy it!"

"I'm going to scrimp and save for the next year so I can buy that."

"If only my _____ would let me do that, I'd buy it for sure."

You feel: Sorry for them, and perhaps like you should reduce your price and help them, or give them money, or a scholarship, or…

What you should do next: The blue light on the Tunometer fades in and out. It's hard for it to have enough energy to stay lit. You need to fade out of this conversation, too. You are not a non-profit organization. Resist the temptation to lower your price in order to be a good person and help the downtrodden. There are charities for that. Don't offer advice unless they have enrolled in your seminar or are paying fees for your coaching. Otherwise, they'll ask you to be their mentor (for free) and you will be receiving long, involved requests for advice forever.

We are all born Tuna Skywalkers, like Luke in *Star Wars*, soft and malleable. Then some grow towards the light and become Dolphin-Wan Kenobi. Others turn to the dark side and become Shark Vader. Your Ometers will help you determine who is who, so you can spend your days swimming with the Dolphins into the light.

Dolphins Sprouting Shark Fins and Teeth

Sometimes people who start out as Dolphins morph into Sharks. This happens because of peer pressure from too many Sharks around them, from losing focus on their core values, getting overwhelmed with bills due to chasing an evermore affluent lifestyle, etc. It happens when corporations restlessly search for more markets, more profits, and ever-increasing dividends for stockholders and are willing to sacrifice their values to get them. It happens when gratitude takes a backseat to greed.

The newspapers are full of stories of corporations that may have started out great but went off the path. I'm sure there were some Dolphins at Enron, World-Com, and the like. But the Shark mentality took over and they plunged into Shark behaviors like lying, cheating, and stealing. A few whistleblower Dolphins led to their downfall, eventually. There were Dolphins who were hurt in the fall, but there were Dolphins that hurt themselves worse before the fall because they gave up their integrity and grew Shark teeth. It's hard to brush those teeth in the morning, remembering when you were proud to be Dr. Dolphin and now you're Mr. Shark Hyde.

> **To all Dolphins in corporations, I give warning: beware when you are asked to fudge the truth, skew the numbers, or take advantage of a Dolphin smaller than you.**

To all Dolphins in corporations, I give warning: beware when you are asked to fudge the truth, skew the numbers, or take advantage of a Dolphin smaller than you. Down that path lies a Shark's feeding frenzy, and you'll never be as vicious a Shark as a real Shark. When the water turns cold, all that remains of the other fish are bones, and finally they turn on each other, you'll be the first to be eaten.

A friend of mine once owned a large mailing service company. A bigger rival wanted to buy her out, but she refused. So they opened up shop next door to her and undercut her prices. They were big enough that they could afford to lose money for a year while they made it difficult for her to stay in business. She capitulated and sold her business. Maybe they won in the short term, and maybe it looks like she lost. But she reopened her real estate business and made a fortune in the next housing boom. I don't know what happened to the mailing company, but with that kind of business model, do you think they could attract loyalty, self sacrificing, fair play, teamwork, or respect from their employees?

> **Pay attention to what your corporations are doing in the name of profit.**

Pay attention to what your corporations are doing in the name of profit. Dolphins have to make judgment calls and stand by their ideals. Do you think it's okay to use child or slave labor in order to knock a dollar off the price for your customers? You cannot abrogate responsibility if you are working for a company that condones practices like that. Or investing in a company with practices like that. Or buying a product that was produced like that.

A Dolphin cares about the community of the world, not just the neighborhood.

How to Handle Dolphin-Shark-Tuna Hybrids

Many people are mixtures of Dolphin-Shark-Tuna. Our Sharkometers aren't always in perfect working order. Sometimes we make an incorrect assessment and then treat someone as a Shark

> **People tend to measure up to your expectation of them.**

who has a lot of Dolphin in them. People tend to measure up to your expectation of them, so if you treat someone like a Shark, they will start behaving like a Shark in your presence. To test the situation, treat them as a Dolphin for a while and see how they respond.

"My husband's a Shark!" exclaimed Margaret. "I have to take your workshop to learn about finances and how to take care of myself because I am probably going to get divorced."

When someone mentions to me that they want to take my Financial Stress Reduction workshop, I ask what specifically it is that they want to change about money in their lives. Often people want more money, more clients in their business, a better job, a bigger house, a nicer car, etc. Margaret wanted these things too, but her biggest stress was in her marriage. She was very unhappy and spoke bitterly about her husband's behavior. She judged him a Shark. She said she had to find out more about how to make and manage money because she was probably going to get divorced.

After the first class of the eight-week session, I took Margaret aside. "I have a suggestion for you," I said. "I don't know you very well and I don't know your husband at all. I'm not a marriage counselor or therapist, but I have a feeling that you might be able to improve things. Are you willing to try?"

"Sure," she said, "Something's got to change."

"Yes," I replied, "and you and I can't change him. But we can change *you*."

Margaret stared at me.

I explained: "The only way that people around you change is

when you change yourself. When you behave in a different way, others will respond differently as well. You have been thinking and saying negative statements like 'My husband's a Shark.' But maybe he's a Dolphin-in-training just having trouble with some of his Sharky bits. Why don't you try doing positive affirmations about your husband instead? There's something good about him, isn't there?"

Wide-eyed, Margaret nodded.

"You can start with 'My husband's a Dolphin.' Treat him like a Dolphin, praise whatever is praiseworthy about him, and stop complaining. He can only act like a Shark when you act as if you're a Tuna."

Margaret committed to this new plan. Her anger abated. She smiled more. By class four, she reported that she had gone over her budgets with her husband. He had been complaining that they didn't have any money and that she spent too much. But with her new financial skills, she went through their finances and showed him that their net worth was nearly a million dollars!

> **When you behave in a different way, others will respond differently as well.**

Margaret's reports about her husband completely changed after that. She started sharing how her husband bought her flowers, told her "I love you," and apologized for not having told her that more often in the past. By the sixth class, she discovered an extra $20,000 in her checking account. When she asked him if he deposited extra money in her account, he admitted that he did. He said that he realized she was right when she complained that he had not been giving her enough money to run the household, so he was making up for it!

At the final class of the workshop, the participants shared what their accomplishments were during the past eight weeks. Margaret looked at her list of "Intended Results." She compared this to her list of accomplishments and said, "I am looking at this list, and I see that I got everything I wrote down here: More money, the certification I need for my new job, clarity about my finances, etc."

She paused thoughtfully, then said, "There's one thing, though, that I didn't get."

All of us looked at her quizzically. What was that?

"A divorce."

Dolphins come in different styles. Just because someone isn't just like you doesn't make them a Shark or a Tuna. They can be a Dolphin, just a different kind of Dolphin. These distinctions aren't to be used to make good people wrong or bad just because they're different. You have to look at their heart and then at their results. If their heart is glad, their ethics are sound, and they produce joy and good in the world, they are Dolphins. Whether they wear sandals, high heels, or gold tennis shoes is just their style.

Attract the People You Want *and* Repel the People You Don't Want

Not only do you want to attract Dolphins, but you want to actually *repel* the Sharks and Tuna. Take a stand for yourself, choose your likes and dislikes, and stand proudly in them. Don't worry about trying to fit in. When you are truly yourself, other people will see it and know you for who you are. This simplifies life immeasurably. Your People will be drawn to you more quickly, and Not Your People run away far and fast. This is a good thing. You don't want your life cluttered up with a bunch of people who don't really like you. It's too much of a time and energy—and money—drain.

I was thinking about this as I drove to the Jonathan Club in downtown Los Angeles to speak to the Los Angeles Chapter of NAWBO (National Association of Women Business Owners). I was dressed in my usual "Give-a-speech-costume"—blouse, blazer, pants, and gold tennis shoes. Gold tennis shoes are part of my brand now—I've been recognized in bookstores because of my shoes. I had a slight hesitation about wearing them to this event since it was a rather corporate environment, but I decided to stick with my usual style.

> **Take a stand for yourself, choose your likes and dislikes, and stand proudly in them. Don't worry about trying to fit in.**

Wouldn't you know, my momentary hesitation manifested itself in a challenge issued to me by one of the Jonathan Club employees in the lobby. "Excuse me, miss," he said frowning disapprovingly at my feet, "but we don't allow tennis shoes in our club."

Oops! Caught already. I grinned up at him and said, "I'm terribly sorry, but I am the speaker this evening and this is my costume."

He wasn't buying it. "Don't you have any other shoes?" he inquired.

"No," I shrugged, "not with me." Oh, dear, I thought, am I going to be thrown out? Barred from the club? My eyes widened and I shifted into sales mode, "You know, I'm sure your dress code means tennis shoes as in *gym* shoes. These are clearly not dirty old gym shoes—they are gold mesh, dressy shoes with diamonds on them."

He paused for a long moment as he thought this over, examining my feet. It must have made sense to him, because he said,

"Okay…but hurry!" He wanted me out of his jurisdiction as soon as possible, and I was happy to oblige him as I scurried upstairs to the meeting room.

The reactions to my gold shoes are always very interesting. Lots of people smile and comment how they just love my shoes, how comfortable they look, etc. I know these are My People. And of course, some people don't like them—one woman told me after the talk that I should dress more professionally if I was going to talk about a serious subject like money. I just smiled, because that's one of the problems I'm trying to solve—that people are too serious about money. Besides, I knew what she did for a living—she sold suits!

People—like shoes—come in different styles. Yvonne Williams, author of *It's All About the Shoes,* told me that women are having their little toes removed so they can wear Jimmy Choo shoes. Ewww. Stop blending in. You are unique. Pick your own style. I remember once walking through the Book Expo in my gold tennies, getting snooty looks from some New York babes-in-black in their pinchy-feet, eight-inch-spike heels. I reveled in it. I'm not part of any matched set. My astrologer promises me that I'm going to become more eccentric. Fabulous! Best news she could give me. Maybe I'll "wear purple and a red hat that doesn't go," too.

But don't judge me until you walk a mile in my gold tennis shoes.

Strategy 5 | Keep Score in the Money Game

"In passing, I've never felt like I could afford a Fender. Even now, there's a strange thing at the back of my mind that makes me think I can't afford a Fender. (Amazing how these things form and stay with you.) A Fender is still a bit of an exotic instrument to me, and even though I could probably afford the factory, it seems out of reach."
—Sir Paul McCartney

Paul's quote perfectly illustrates how your feelings about money can be rooted in your past and don't necessarily reflect your current reality. Sarah Jessica Parker was interviewed on television when she was in the middle of her great success with *Sex and the City*. Yet she talked about growing up very poor and how she still felt nervous about money, that it could all suddenly disappear, like water down a drain. Like these celebrities, if you don't consciously work to change your old ideas about having money, you could remain mentally stuck in a reality you left long ago.

But the discipline and commitment of these artists to their purpose led them to phenomenal success, in spite of their holdover feelings of financial inadequacy. Their focus on where they were going, rather than on where they were or where they had been, kept them moving forward towards the prosperity they desired. What usually lifts successful people out of their beginning poorer circumstances is the passion they feel for their purpose. It's not all about the money and things they might acquire, but rather about the freedom to pursue the path they have chosen—so they can do the work they believe they are meant to do.

But passion is not enough. Passion must be harnessed to discipline. Tiger Woods had to practice his golf swing, Mikhail Baryshnikov had to take ballet classes, Mariah Carey had to vocalize and exercise her five-octave range. We have raw talents, but to hone them takes discipline. Then we must make our skills known in the marketplace—another discipline. We have to reach out beyond the reality we know to the success we desire. We have to think positive every day and send out our ships to reach our goals. We have to learn to swim with Dolphins. Then, if we want to achieve *financial* success, we have to add this next step: count our money. The money is the score of the game and the amount of money we create will tell us how well we're doing at the other success strategies.

Minding Your Money without Losing Your Mind

"I've just always been math-challenged," my client Sandra moaned. "The words *balance sheet* and *income statement* scare me! I don't know how or where to start doing the accounting for my business."

I certainly understand her predicament. My clients often look scared and unhappy when we face accounting. I've been there myself. Accounting didn't come naturally to me, either.

I was good at the liberal arts subjects: English, art, music, dance, drama. All through high school, and as a drama major in college, I avoided math like the plague. Math class in my day had word problems that began, "Farmer John has six bushes of wheat and he sells them at thirty-nine cents a bushel…" Uh, who's Farmer John? What's a bushel? When's recess? I just couldn't relate. So I tuned out and turned off.

It wasn't until I was working as a secretary and the company promoted me to Office Manager that I had to learn it, because bookkeeping was one of my duties. I told them I didn't know anything about it, but they said they'd teach me. So I nervously set out to learn what I had been avoiding all these years—and was amazed to discover I loved it. It wasn't "accounting"—it was "counting my money." Like Cuba Gooding's character in *Jerry Maguire*, everyone in the company came to me and said, "Show me the money!" They were all bringing money in or sending money out, and some of that money was mine. The life of the business depended on making sure there was more money coming in than going out. That's what profit is, and without profit, eventually there won't be any business, and then everyone is out of a job.

You can learn all the accounting you need to be successful. If I could learn it, you can, too. You can be financially successful. You can get the results you want—money in the bank, work you love, fat savings accounts, zero debt, wonderful vacation trips, beautiful homes, clothes, cars, cash, and control over your money and your life. You can have the money you want to do the things you want. You just have to design the plan to have them.

> **You can learn all the accounting you need to be successful.**

Between where you are now and your vision of your prosperous future, you need the discipline to do the work. There are too many people who learn what to do but don't do it. Knowing about it and doing it are two different things.

The program works. It can work for you. But you have to work it. You can have success or failure—your choice. Are you ready?

Baby-U-Deserve-Getting-Every-Thing (Budget)

We keep track of the score of the money game on the money score-card—the budget.

What's your response to the word *budget*? Do you have a sinking, shrinking, depressed feeling? Are you afraid if you count the money you're going to find that you can't afford the lifestyle you've become accustomed to? Or want to become accustomed to? Do you think your money will somehow work out all right if you just don't look at it too closely? Are you Cleopatra, the Queen of Denial?

> **If you don't count your money, you are always going to be stressed about money.**

Let me give you a tip: if you don't count your money, you are always going to be stressed about money. You won't ever be relaxed, or feel secure or rich. You will always have a gnawing sensation that maybe some bill is coming due that you've forgotten. You won't know if you can afford to take that great vacation trip to Italy, or buy that gold watch, or how much of a mortgage you can handle. You'll drug yourself with the credit card crack so often the thought of sobriety will scare you silly. Visit a Debtors Anonymous meeting if you don't believe me.

So first, we have to make friends with the word *budget*.

Relax. This isn't advanced calculus, algebra, geometry, or trig. This is one-plus-one stuff, and if you can't count that, how do you expect to count your millions? I heard recently that a woman reading a newspaper with the headline "Twelve Brazilian Soldiers

Wounded" turned to her companion and asked, "How many is in a Brazilian?"

Budgets give you grounding in reality, like a scale does for a dieter. Only the dieter wants to see a lower number and we want to see a higher one. If you don't count, you won't know where you are in your program. You won't know if it's working or not, or if it is producing the results you want.

One woman in my workshop came to class after doing her budgets and said, "The good news is I doubled my income last year."

Everyone in the room cheered.

"What's the bad news?" I asked.

"The bad news is I only increased my profit two percent."

It often happens that when we start making more money, we get uncomfortable. We don't know what to do with the extra money, so we get rid of it in order to return to our comfort zone. Yes, for some people, being broke and anxious can be the comfort zone. If she had been budgeting every month, she would have seen the path she was headed down sooner and been able to take steps to reduce her spending before all that extra money was gone.

Budgeting can be fun when you discover that you are making more money and enjoying more riches. Then you can carefully plan what you want to do with your excess cash. Isn't

> Yes, for some people, being broke and anxious can be the comfort zone.

that a great expression? I want you to have plenty of excess cash. Then your only problem will be what to do with it all. As your life improves, it doesn't mean you won't have problems—just that the quality of your problems will improve. I want to have High Class Quality Problems, like what to do with all my excess cash. How about you?

But you won't have any extra money unless you budget. It will disappear into the black holes of the Universe that suck up all the excess cash that people haven't budgeted. If you don't have a plan for it, it will disappear. That's why so many lotto winners end up broke within five years. We shake our heads over these stories, but these poor folks have no idea how to be rich. They have no consciousness about how to manage large sums of money, so they spend it foolishly, give large sums away to family and friends, go on spending binges, and forget that they are going to owe taxes or that they've incurred debts that are going to catch up with them next year. If you've always lived paycheck to paycheck, what's natural for you is to be scrambling to pay your bills. So that is the situation that they unconsciously set up for themselves to be in again. They're still broke—they're just broke at a higher level. If your unconscious habit is to spend more than you make, it won't matter how much you make. You'll always find a way to spend more.

> **Budgeting can be fun when you discover that you are making more money and enjoying more riches.**

The only way out of the trap is to create budgets to plan your spending. Not just for the way things are right now, with your current income and expenses, but with contingency plans attached. What if you made more money? What would you spend it on? What if you made less money? What would you do without?

Some financial planners try to avoid using the word budget and disguise it in more user-friendly verbiage like "spending plan" or "savings plan." It doesn't work. You know they're talking about a budget. So I have reframed the meaning of the word: I say it stands for "Baby-U-Deserve-Getting-Every-Thing." Now saying "budget" is like saying a positive affirmation. A budget is your declaration of your priorities for spending your money. Get happy with budgets, because they are your navigational chart to riches.

You are going to need three different budgets. I have complicated names for them: Low, Medium, and High. Each of these is a budget for one month. You design all three and then at the beginning of each month, you choose which budget you are on for the coming month. Anyone can be on Low Budget for a month! That's as long a commitment as you have to make. Be committed for one month, be disciplined for one month. Then perhaps next month you can move up to Medium Budget. Maybe you'll get a raise or a promotion. Maybe you'll get a diamond in your downline. Maybe you'll get a $7 million contract. Lastly, you need to look ahead to what's in your High Budget. What are you going to buy when your big ship comes in? High Budget is a positive affirmation in action. Because if you don't have a reason to spend the money, you won't have a reason to make the money.

> **You are going to need three different budgets. I have complicated names for them: Low, Medium, and High.**

Medium Budget for Middle Money

Prepare this budget first. This is the budget for the way things are for you financially right now. What is your actual monthly income? What are you spending it on? Make a list of all income sources, and then list all your monthly expenses.

If you are employed, you know exactly how much money you make, so the income portion on your budget is whatever your monthly salary is. If you are self-employed or work on commission, you have to guess what it is going to be. Business owners are always complaining to me that they know how much money they spend, but they never know how much money they're going to make. I tell them, "You have to know!" You don't get to spend money you aren't committed to making. I tell them to go back and count up their total income for the last twelve months and then divide by twelve. That will be the estimated income for budgeting purposes. If they bank the extra during the fat months, they'll be able to draw on it during the lean months. The trick for everyone is to keep your expenses below your income. You'll always have extra money to save, use for emergencies, or splurge.

Permission to splurge on occasion is your divine right. Each of the three budgets has to have a category for "Splurge Money." Just splurge within the appropriate budget, so you don't end up washed away in a sea of red ink. Black is beautiful.

Low Budget Is Only for One Month

The next budget to prepare is Low Budget. This is the Bad News Budget, the lack and limitation budget. This is the budget everyone fears—the one that tells you that you can't have things, that you can't spend the money, because you "can't afford it." But remember, this budget is just for one month. It's only when you think Low Budget is forever that it's depressing. After you prepare it, your Medium Budget will look great by comparison, and you will feel more abundant. If you're on Low Budget now, we're going to chart the course to get you off of it and up the food chain as soon as possible.

First of all, never say you "can't afford it" again. That's negative thinking, and it's not true. It's just that at this precise moment you are unwilling to allocate your resources to that particular item, because there are other things you want more. Say, "That isn't my budget priority right now" instead. That's a more accurate statement and it feels more empowering to say it that way. All budget categories are choices.

Create Low Budget by carefully examining every item in your Medium Budget. Identify which items you could do without for a month and put a zero in the expense column for those items. Maybe you will eliminate spending money on clothes, or dinners at restaurants, or going to the movies. Take out every item you can live without for a month. Then look at categories you can spend less on, and reduce the amount of money—just for this month—that you will spend on them.

I know this is hard. I have sat with many people over the years as they struggled with their budgets. They painted themselves into a corner and they couldn't see the bridge over the red ink sea. I'm not sitting with each of you reading this book, but pretend that I am. I'm going to ask you to justify every expense. And then I'll tell you that you don't have to spend that much, if at all. Try again. Start over.

Many immigrants start out as street peddlers, says Gwen Kinkead in *From Chinatown: A Portrait of a Closed Society*. She tells how they live frugally and in three or four years often save as much as $50,000 $100,000. They are able to do this because they have a commitment to saving in order to accumulate the capital to start a business. One man, Mr. Lin, sold fruit, vegetables, and umbrellas, making an average of $22,000 a year, of which he saved $18,000. He spent money only on rent, telephone, and food. "Rice very cheap," he said, smiling.

With this in mind, take another look at your budget now. Think you can trim it a bit more?

Spending money is a habit. And that's a habit you'll be breaking when you're on Low Budget. It teaches you the lesson of frugality, how to not spend, how to make do with what you already possess, how to have fun with the "best things in life"—which are free, if

Spending money is a habit.

you'll remember. Take every bit of frill and fluff out of your spending plans. See what you can do without. Not for your lifetime— just for one month.

Sometimes we are so rooted in our habits and justifications for our expenses, we forget that we chose them and that there are other options available.

When I coached Monica, she told me that she couldn't find anything else to cut out of her budget, yet she was only earning $3,000 per month but spending $4,000. I looked at her budget and said, "What about $200 a month for books and tapes? That could be reduced to zero."

"Absolutely not!" she exclaimed. "That's for my education and my spiritual growth!"

"Books are free at the library," I said. "Or borrow the books from your friends."

"Oh. I didn't think of that," she replied sheepishly. We were then able to make additional cuts until we got her budget balanced.

Some of the people I work with don't appreciate hearing the truth about their situation. I don't just get wonderful success letters—I've gotten nasty letters, too. One woman wrote to me requesting a refund six months after the class was over because she had forgotten that affirmations didn't work for everyone, and obviously she was one of those people because she wasn't better off financially.

Sorry, but my job as a teacher isn't to be everyone's best friend, although I certainly like it when that happens. Sometimes my job is to hold up the mirror and show them what they're doing to themselves, even if it makes them angry at me. So I wrote her back that the tools of the class do work and have worked for thousands of people. But affirmations are only one of the tools. Her real problems lay in her budget, and I told her what they were:

1. Her children were in private school and she didn't have the income to pay for that. ("But my children's education is the most important thing in the world!" she exclaimed when I told her to transfer them to public school or find a less expensive private school.)

2. She had moved into a new house that added hundreds of dollars to her rent. ("But we had to move and this was a great deal!")

3. She didn't increase her income by asking for a raise, getting another part-time job, or reducing other expenses on her budget. ("I'm looking for another job, but there just aren't any that are right for me.")

Did you notice all the "yeah, buts"? I wished her well and hoped that she would be able to turn her finances around. And no, I didn't give her a refund.

No affirmation in the world is going to solve the above problems. They are solved by earning more money, spending less money, or finding a creative way to have what you want. The Zillionaire program is like

> **The Zillionaire program is like the recipe for cake—you have to put *all* the ingredients in.**

the recipe for cake—you have to put *all* the ingredients in. You can't leave out the eggs and then complain that the recipe was no good because your soufflé turned out flat. Don't blame the author of the cookbook if you don't follow the directions.

If you are in trouble financially, and there isn't enough money to make ends meet, you have to take radical action to change. It begins with taking full and complete responsibility for your problems—that *you* set them up and *you* perpetuate them. If you do that and then work the plan I am presenting in this book, your financial problems will be solved. Positive thinking just helps you get in the right frame of mind to work on them. When you are willing to face these truths, you will be able to take the actions you need to turn your situation around. When you are willing to take 100 percent responsibility that everything that happens to you is either your fault or to your credit, then change can happen. Until then you will blame the affirmations, the book, me, your boss, your landlord, the government, et al for your problems. But you can't change any of us. You can only change you. It's all you. And when you change, your finances will change.

> **When you are willing to take 100 percent responsibility that everything that happens to you is either your fault or to your credit, then change can happen.**

Remember that Low Budget is not forever. Lighten up about it and make it a game! Who do you know who might invite you out for dinner—and pick up the check? Who has something you want who might want something you have? Look for opportunities to trade or barter services. What work can you do part-time that would also bring in extra cash? What can you fix instead of buying new? Create new outfits to wear by mixing and matching things from the back of your closet. And each day you succeed in conserving your cash with creative ideas, congratulate yourself on your wisdom and money mastery.

Go shopping—not spending. I mean window shopping. Leave your cash, checks, and credit cards at home. Go to the mall and visit the stuff you're going to get when you're on High Budget. Make lists of items and their prices. Then add it all up when you get home and celebrate: "Woo hoo! Saved forty thousand dollars today!" Every dollar you don't spend is a dollar that is still in your pocket.

Happiness is making $1000 and spending $900. Misery is making $1000 and spending $1100. Which do you choose?

Budget Busters: The Irregular Expenses

Before we get to the fun—creating High Budget—there is a Part II for all of these budgets that we need. This is the Irregular Expenses Budget.

Some people design mighty fine budgets that have all their regular monthly expenses listed in neat little rows, and still end up in debt. That's because there are expenses that are a part of everyone's budget but they are irregular—they don't occur every month—so we forget them. They only come due in certain months, or once a year: property taxes, insurance payments, Christmas presents, vacation expenses, auto repairs, additional income taxes, quarterly tax deposits for the self-employed, professional dues, birthday bashes, etc. From time to time, houses need new roofs, you have to visit the dentist, it's time to buy a new car or a new computer.

How many times have you been going along just fine paying all your bills and starting to get ahead, when all of a sudden—boom! The car breaks down and needs a new gizmo to the tune of $500. Or the plumbing backs up, the water heater breaks, the computer gets a virus—or you do. If only you had known that was going to happen last week, before you went shopping and splurged. Now what?

To prevent the unexpected from blowing a black hole in your budget, you need to create a list of all the irregular expenses you can think of that are likely to happen during the year, with a reserve amount for the unlikely. Write down the actual cost if you know it, or guestimate the cost if you don't. If you have an old car, put down some amount for repairs. If you have a new car, put down an amount for maintenance. If you have children, put down a significant amount for extra things your kids are likely to need without warning: school activities, clubs, hobbies, sports equipment, dance classes, trips, etc. After you list everything you can think of, total the amounts, then divide by twelve. This is the additional amount you need to put in your budget under expenses.

Now open up a separate money market account and deposit the monthly amount of your irregular expenses in that account each month. For example, if all your irregular expenses totaled $6,000 for the year, you would deposit $500 per month in this account. Then, whenever one of these expenses comes up, you can pay for it right out of your special account. I recommend adding some additional money into it as an extra buffer—what a client of mine called her REFOO money. When I asked her what REFOO stood for, she said, "REserved For Over Optimism." Or it can be extra splurge money or extra savings, too, depending on how well you count your money.

Big Bad Budget Buster: Debt

There are two kinds of debt—good debt and bad debt.

Good debt is when you get a loan from the Small Business Administration or a bank to start your own business. Good debt is arranging a low-interest-rate mortgage so you can buy a home or income property. Good debt is what you borrow to invest in asset building for your financial future. It is leveraging other people's money to help you make more money.

Bad Debt weighs on people like sixteen tons. It beats them down, creating its own negative energy, leading them to say, "What's the use? I'm never going to get ahead." They feel guilty and depressed, and to escape, they go shopping. They splurge on something they know they can't afford, and that makes them feel good for about a minute and a half. Then they feel guilty and even more depressed. Their debts grow larger.

> **Bad Debt weighs on people like sixteen tons.**

The average American owes about $8,000–10,000 on credit cards alone. Add in car loans, mortgages, and school loans, and the numbers are overwhelming. It's difficult to stay in a positive frame of mind when you face your debts. For most people, debt becomes a nagging worry that hangs over them at all times. They start channeling their Inner Homeless Person, who points a bony finger and predicts a dreary life of dusty streets and shopping carts ahead. Sharks gather, smelling blood in the water. This is a typical Tuna scenario.

But even if you have been a Tuna in the past, you are a Dolphin-in-training now. You can escape all this debt and the negative thinking that perpetuates it. You have debt because you have negative thinking, not vice versa. When your thinking is stinking, you send out black plague ships instead of treasure galleons. So what do you think they're going to be unloading at your dock?

Your current debt is merely a reflection of bad thinking and bad habits in your past. You may have lost your job, lost a big client, or had a major medical expense, or a family member has had one of these problems. You may have overspent your income, paid too much for houses, cars, clothes, vacations, etc. You may have resigned yourself to a low-paying job, all the while hungering for a high-budget lifestyle. You know what you did that put you in the pickle you're in.

> **Your current debt is merely a reflection of bad thinking and bad habits in your past.**

It doesn't matter how you got there. Now it's time to get out. You have to think like a Zillionaire, that you are rich and wonderful, and double up on all your abundance affirmations. Stop the negative thinking. Put "debt reduction" as a line item in your budget and create a plan to pay them off. Then follow the plan religiously. Celebrate every time you make a payment on your debts. See yourself getting wealthier with every dollar you pay to reduce your debt. Count the debts at the end of every month and see the number getting smaller. You won't have trouble thinking positive about *that*!

Even if you are in debt and on Low Budget, you still need to save money. Most financial advisors will tell you to pay off debt first, and then start your savings plan, and this makes sense from a mathematical point of view. But human beings are creatures of habit, and if you don't start the savings habit now, you won't ever do it. On any budget. Because you will keep increasing your expenses as you increase your income. You have to get into the habit of saving. Make saving money a part of the plan right now, even if it doesn't look like there is enough money for that. Have the intention and make the commitment to save, and more money will show up.

Let me give you a tip: the extra money for savings doesn't show up at the end of the month. There's always too much month left at the end of the money. That's why your commitment to savings has to take place at the *beginning* of the month. Make a deposit to savings when you write out your rent or mortgage check. Transfer a portion to savings every time you deposit your paycheck or a client's payment. Then you will do what is necessary to make sure you create enough income to pay your bills during the rest of the month. You may get better at controlling your spending urges then, too.

> Let me give you a tip: the extra money for savings doesn't show up at the end of the month. There's always too much month left at the end of the money. That's why your commitment to savings has to take place at the beginning of the month.

Here's a wake up call: Add up all the money you've earned in the last ten or twenty years. Pretty big number, eh? Now add up the total amount of your savings, retirement accounts, and the worth of your assets (above what you owe on them). How much is that? What percentage of the total amount of money you have made in your life do you still have?

If you don't have any savings and you have debt, it's just that you were never taught how to create a different habit with money. But now you are learning it. Forgive yourself for the wreckage of the past, and congratulate yourself for the bright shining future you have started creating today. Remember that your debt is just a number on a piece of paper. It isn't you, it isn't your spirit, it isn't your future. Zero debt is your future. You are a Zillionaire, on your way to making zillions.

High Budget Moves Your Bottom Line to the Top of the Line

Now you get to design your High Budget—this is your Zillionaire Budget, your budget for living The Good Life. Don't wait until you have more money. Creating High Budget now will help you make more money. Besides, it's fun! This is your goal for spending money—what do you want to have and do when you're on High Budget? Get pictures and brochures of the things you really want and put them on your wall—some people call this a "Treasure Map" or a "Dream Board." Start a special savings plan for major purchases. Be specific: If you want a new car, what make, model, and color is it? What features and options does it have? Smile and feel the pleasure now as if you already owned it. Spend some time each day looking at it and feeling rich. Affirm your ability to create this abundance in your life. If you continue to visualize it, plan for it, save for it, budget it, and think up creative ways to make more money to pay for it, it won't be long before you have it.

When you are on High Budget, you have to change the habits that you developed when you were on Low Budget and had to learn how to control your spending. Now you have room to expand your reality and the flow of money. You have to change your mindset and think rich instead of poor.

And you have to stop being cheap.

I don't mean to blow all your money foolishly, of course. But there is such a thing as spending anorexia. (There may be income bulimia, too, but no one who has it complains about it.) You must develop the ability to spend money happily. On any budget, you will need to pay top dollar for some things, because in some instances, quality matters more than price. Years ago, a group of people quit a networking group I belonged to because they said it was too expensive. They wanted to help people network at more reasonable prices, and solicited everyone to come join them in their new, cheaper network. They got a lot of people to join them, too—all the people with money problems. So most of the people there couldn't afford to buy anyone else's products and services. Not to mention the organizers weren't making very much money themselves. The group disbanded after a year or two. It reminded me of the time when I joined a dating service that cost $1,000. Some people exclaimed that was too much money and joined a cheaper service. That's fine, I said, but I want to meet men who have the motivation and money to join an *expensive* dating service. The price of a service is sometimes a great screening device.

> **You must develop the ability to spend money happily. On any budget, you will need to pay top dollar for some things, because in some instances, quality matters more than price.**

Aside from being willing and knowing when to pay more for quality, it is important to have extra money with which to bless others—in all your transactions, not just in giving to charity. Charitable contribution should be on all of your budgets and escalate as your situation improves. But when you're on High Budget, you don't always have to shop during the sale, drive twenty miles to get the discount, or drive the hardest bargain in a negotiation. You can loosen up. Appreciate the *outflow* of money, too. When you buy things from other people, you are sending ships into their harbors. Enjoy making other people rich and happy. That's when you know you are living rich—inside and out—and fear of financial insecurity fades away like a ship's horn on a foggy night.

One afternoon, I had a nice lunch with an accountant. Afterwards, we went outside to collect our cars from the valet. He pointed to the posted sign that said "Valet Parking $1.75" and complained, "I just hate that price. You know they're just trying to get that extra quarter out of you."

I looked at him in amazement. "You're not only going to tip a quarter, are you?" I said. "Loosen up. Give the valet three dollars!"

> **Enjoy making other people rich and happy. That's when you know you are living rich—inside and out—and fear of financial insecurity fades away.**

Too much focus on getting a discount, buying on sale, finding low cost services, or driving a hard bargain doesn't make you feel richer; it just reinforces a poverty mentality that has outlived its usefulness. I heard a story about one of the world's richest men, Warren Buffett. Years ago, a friend (I think it was Barbara Walters) asked him for a dime to make a phone call in a phone booth. All he had was a quarter. Reluctant to part with it because a phone call only cost a dime in those days, he started looking around for change. "Warren, just give me the quarter!" ribbed his exasperated friend. This is a perfect example of someone who was excruciatingly careful of their money when they were building their assets and just couldn't quite let go of the habit when they became rich.

Save Money and Enjoy Life, Too

All these financial professionals whose books, magazines, newsletters, CDs, etc. exhort you to stop spending money on lattes and save your pennies seem to have missed the news that pennies aren't worth squat anymore. It's understandable because they make their living from getting you to save and invest your money with them rather than spend it on yourself. That is fine up to a point. We have to make sure that we have some money tucked away for the future when we might like to retire or not work as many hours empire-building as we did when we were young. But twenty-nine people out of one hundred die before they reach retirement age. We've got to have some balance in the program and spend some of our money enjoying life now.

My father worked and saved all his life, building equity in his home and a pension when he retired from his company, and carefully increasing his savings and assets. When he was eighty-four, he sold the family home he had lived in for forty-six years. My sisters and I discussed different housing options with him and looked at retirement communities, condos, and assisted living facilities. He was very concerned about his budget, preserving his savings, and not spending too much money. I nudged him and said, "Dad, all your life you have done a great job at saving for your retirement. Well, this is it! This is the retirement you've been saving for. You get to change your habit now and spend the money." We laughed about it, but old habits die hard. And it feels so good and safe to have money saved, it's difficult to let go of it.

Be wise with your money. Save some, but not too much. Spend some, but not too much. Sometimes getting control over your money means pulling back. Sometimes it means loosening up. You need to be able to do both, and adjust what you do depending on your current circumstances. The fringe positions—all savings or all spending, all black or all white—are never the positions that work well in life or money. A balanced life and a balanced checkbook mean negotiating the gray areas in the middle. Look at your budgets over the next few months and see what adjustments are best for you right now.

Then keep looking. And keep adjusting. It's a process. The more you do it, the easier it gets, and the more money flows more easily to you. And the more money you get, the more fun it is to play with your budgets!

Budget with Your Children

Design a budget for your children with your children. Yes, with their active participation. It will teach your kids about how money is made and give them some power and responsibility over their own spending. Make a list of what chores are worth and let them earn their allowance. They need to see that service (i.e., work) equals money. Otherwise they don't understand why you don't just go to the ATM when you run out of money.

A delightful couple in my workshop, Kat Kehres and Curtis Knecht, had recently married. Each had two children from a prior marriage, and they planned a first vacation to bond their blended family. But only a couple of days into the trip, everyone was frazzled and fighting over what to do and how to spend their limited budget. What was going wrong?

When Kat and Curtis had started planning their vacation, there were many emotional, financial, and logistical issues to consider. They knew that money could be a disruptive force, and that their children had different expectations and experiences of what a vacation was.

They were afraid that this could create a strain on them and make the kids feel miserable. So they used what they had learned about affirming a positive outcome and created a budget for the vacation. They wanted the limits set in their budget to free them from making spending decisions from an emotionally chaotic place. They planned every detail of the trip from the moment they left home. They decided what kind of restaurants and how many side trips and included spending money for the children.

The very first dinner got off to a rocky start, with tears shed over what they had allowed the kids to order. The dream of the trip being a bonding experience now looked a little lofty. They realized they needed to include the kids in the plan. The next day, they showed the children the budget so that they would all be on the same page. They divided up the spending money and let them each be in charge of how they would spend it, including snacks, activities, souvenirs, and everything other than three meals and a roof. This gave the children freedom of choice, gave the parents freedom from persistent requests, and united them all in a surprising way. Once they had the money in their pockets, the kids suddenly discovered ways to have fun that didn't cost a penny. They ended up doing stuff together instead of relying on bought entertainment. Everyone learned something from this.

The children joined in playing with the monetary limits they had set as their plans changed. On the last night, they chose to eat sandwiches in their room so that they all could afford to be together in a hotel where they could have fun swimming, playing Yahtzee, and enjoying a great big breakfast before ending the trip.

Children can be wiser than you know. Guide them rather than order them.

It became a magical trip, where everyone got what he or she wanted. Their kids bonded in ways Kat and Curtis had not even imagined. They had the opportunity to enjoy this new family in a way that was relaxed and fun. They saw the power and fun in choosing to use money as a creative, positive energy.

Children can be wiser than you know. Give them a chance to show you. Give them some power, some control, some acknowledgment. Guide them rather than order them. They will take these lessons with them into the future. They will develop respect for the earning of money and the spending of it as well.

Magic Money Wish List

I invented the "Magic Money Wish List" when I found there were things I wanted to buy that I hadn't budgeted for on any of my Low, Medium, High, or Irregular Budgets. You know what I'm talking about: a sparkly new party dress, a quick weekend out-of-town getaway, some new sports equipment, a new software program for the computer, a new bedroom set, an educational seminar, etc. When I started making a list of these things as goals, the money to buy them wasn't readily available. I just had the intention that the money would show up somehow.

Would you like some Magic Money in your life? For what? Write it down. Intend to have it.

And the money came. One by one, I crossed things off the list. Finally, after I had about three pages of these things crossed off, I realized I had created an exercise that worked, so I started to share it in my workshops. I wrote a page about it in my first book, and I often get letters from people about how it worked for them.

One woman wrote to say that after she read about the Magic Money List, she wrote down that she needed $245. Then she drove off to meet a friend for lunch. At the end of the lunch, her friend said she had inherited a little money, and handed her a check for $300. After that, she wrote down that she wanted $100 for some auto repairs. She later visited her brother, who handed her an envelope with a $100 bill in it.

The letter went on, but you get the drift. Would you like some Magic Money in your life? For what? Write it down. Intend to have it. Affirm it. Open to receive it. Expect it. And watch "out-of-the-blue" Magic Money arrive.

How to Ask for a Raise and Get It

"I'm going to ask for a raise," I declared to my co-worker and friend Jennifer.

"Yeah? Why do you think you deserve one?" she asked.

I was incensed. What did she mean? Wasn't she my friend?

"Well, I've been here a year already," I huffed.

"So what? Just warming the bench doesn't mean you deserve more money," she replied.

Tuna Chellie frowned and looked at her resentfully.

"Come with me," she said, and motioned for me to sit down in her office. Then she taught me what I needed to know.

"Asking for a raise is just like making a sale," Jennifer said. She went on to explain that you have to list all your accomplishments and what they mean to the company in terms of producing or saving money. Just doing an acceptable job at what you were hired to do doesn't mean you deserve more money. Raises come to people who have done an exceptional job and have worked at a level beyond the scope of their current job. She showed me how to compare how things were at the company when I arrived, how I have improved them, and what they are like now. She told me to research other com-

Asking for a raise is just like making a sale.

panies and what they were paying people in similar jobs. Armed with this new sales technique, I went in to see the boss, closed the sale, and got a raise.

That was many years ago, but I never forgot Jennifer's training, and I know a lot of people never had a Jennifer in their life to share with them this valuable lesson. It's another sales lesson. Whether you're asking a boss for a raise or raising your rates to your clients, you have to make the sale. Paint the picture of how much you have done in the past and what you are going to do in the future to make their lives better and more prosperous, so that they can see you deserve more money.

You have to get comfortable with earning more money and being more abundant. Practice saying your new salary or your new price so that you can say it without hesitation. If you think it's a big number, your awe will show, and people will talk you out of it. Often people who have rich clients are afraid to ask for a reasonable amount of money for their products or services. A massage therapist might feel awkward charging $125 for a massage if he couldn't afford it himself.

A Little Exercise to Enlarge Your Income

Here's something to practice that could greatly increase your income. Let's say that your current price for your product or service is one hundred dollars and you'd like to start charging one hundred fifty dollars. For you to say, "I charge one hundred fifty dollars" after you've been saying "one hundred dollars" for a long while is difficult. It's uncomfortable because you're in the habit of saying one hundred dollars. All your fears about your worthiness and ability to receive abundance clutch at your insides. You choke on the words, stutter, or make your request weakly, wincing while you say, "I, uh, charge, er, a hundred and um, ah, fifty dollars?"

The client is going to call that obvious bluff immediately: "A hundred and fifty dollars?! That's too much money!" That will never do.

You've got to say your new price proudly and strongly. You have to *practice* saying it, so that you can toss the figure away when you say it, like you think it's nothing. Here's the trick that will help: take the new price (not the current price) you want to charge—one hundred fifty dollars—and double that to three hundred dollars. Sounds outrageous, doesn't it? That's the point. Now practice saying that price: "I charge three hundred dollars, I charge three hundred dollars," over and over, at least twenty times a day for a week or two. You will be amazed at how little one hundred fifty dollars sounds to you after that. You'll speak it easily to your clients, because after three hundred dollars, one hundred fifty dollars sounds like a bargain. Your clients will take their cue from you this time, too, and be more likely to have a more relaxed acceptance of your price.

> You've got to say your new price proudly and strongly. You have to practice saying it, so that you can toss the figure away when you say it, like you think it's nothing.

Many of my clients have been amazed at how well this exercise has worked for them. Not only that, but a lot of them reported their clients mentioned being surprised their prices had been so low and were *waiting* for them to start charging a higher rate.

The Small Business Administration reports that one of the top reasons small businesses go under is that they don't charge enough money for their products or services. My client, Adi, taught all-day yoga classes and charged six dollars. He got ten students, one of whom didn't even pay the six dollars. He knew his pricing was too low, but he just enjoyed teaching the class and didn't want money to stand in the way of people attending. But he needed more money in his life, so he decided to charge $235 for the next all-day session. He got three students. In the first scenario, he made $54. In the second, he made $705. The difference in his income was $651.

How Much Money Do You Want?

I give myself a raise every year or so. If I were working for someone else, I'd want a raise, and I want to be a better boss to myself than someone else would. A lot of entrepreneurs who don't pay themselves enough money would never work for such a chintzy boss in the corporate world. In fifteen years of teaching classes, I have found that how much I charge makes no difference in attendance at my workshops. It makes a difference in *who* attends, not how many attend. There are about twenty million people in the greater Los Angeles area, and I don't need all of them—I only need twelve. So I call until I get twelve—you see? If I charged less, in order to make the same income, I would have to enroll many more people. Then I would have to book a hotel instead of doing it at my house, which would cost more money, so I'd need to enroll more people, and then I'd need more help and then I'd have to have employees and then I'd have to enroll more people to pay the employees, and then it's a bigger business than I want. And I've lost the life I want.

But the sales process for my workshop business—the enrollment conversation—takes the same amount of time, no matter what my price is. That's why bankers don't bother with small loans—it takes them the same amount of time to process a $10,000 loan as a $10 million loan and they make a lot more money on the bigger loan. In the same way, I want to make sure the pricing works for me, first. You need to start with your vision, then work backwards to see what you need to charge in order to create your living the way you want to live your life. If people want the benefits of what you do, they will pay the price for it, whatever it is. There will always be people who "can't afford you." You can't bring your pricing down to the lowest common denominator and only charge a dollar because there are poor people who need you who only have a dollar. You can run a charity like that, but you can't run a business like that. Don't choose a nonprofit business model unless you're a bona-fide 501c3.

> **You need to start with your vision, then work backwards to see what you need to charge in order to create your living the way you want to live your life.**

Whatever price you choose, there will always be people who complain about the price. There were people who complained about the price of my class when it was $450 and there were people who complained about it when it was $850, then $1200, then $1500, etc. Someone even posted a review of *The Wealthy Spirit* on Amazon.com to complain, "It's a big turn-off that this author is charging and receiving great amounts of money for her seminars." Really? How could you expect me to teach you how to be wealthy if I don't charge good prices and make good money myself? But that's a typical Angry Tuna response. A Dolphin-in-training response would be, "Wow, she is able to charge that much and get it? I'm going to sign up because I want to learn how to do that!"

One of my mentors, Patty DeDominic, taught me an important principle about raising prices: "If you're going to raise your prices, raise them a lot. People will complain about a one-dollar increase just as much as a five-dollar increase, so make it worth your while." She added that you'll always lose a few clients at the bottom of the scale who can't pay more or don't want to, but the additional money you'll make from the rest paying the higher prices will more than make up for that. You'll work fewer hours and make more money.

> **Whatever price you choose, there will always be people who complain about the price.**

Audrey was a hairstylist taking my class, and her prices were way below market, but week after week, I just couldn't convince her to raise them. "Oh, but my clients can't afford more than twenty-five dollars," she would say. "Sure they can," I encouraged her. "Or you can get richer clients. I was paying more than twenty-five dollars for a haircut in 1975!" Her eyes widened at that, but she stubbornly clung to her pricing, even though she wasn't making enough money. She was afraid she would lose the customers she had, and she needed every one of them in order to pay her bills. It was hard for her to have faith that, even with all the people in Los Angeles, there would be enough people willing to pay her higher prices.

She kept doing her affirmations, networking to find new clients, and did some market research on pricing. Finally, she agreed that she could raise her prices—to twenty-eight dollars, an increase of three dollars. I sighed. "Okay," I said, "It's a start. Congratulations on being willing to take the risk."

Yes, we want to be smart shoppers, and yes, we want to be careful with our budgets, but we needn't get into such a habit that we're always trying to shave a dollar or two off a price when it really doesn't matter that much to us. Spending anorexia is a money disorder, too.

Pricing to Make Your Business Profitable

If you're working in a home-based business or plan to, you need to become proficient at counting your money. Keep it simple—list all your income from your business each month at the top of a piece of paper. This is your gross. Then list all the expenses related to your business. When you subtract the money you spent from the money you made, you have your profit or net. (My friend and accountant, Barbara Barschak, has an easy method for remembering the difference between gross and net: net is a smaller word.) You can do a simple spreadsheet or you can use an accounting software package.

Here is the reason you do all this counting: look at your "net" and see if that's the amount of money you want to be making every month. If the figure is too low, you need to raise your prices, make more sales, or make bigger sales to bigger customers. Or perhaps your income is fine, but you're spending too much money on new computer programs, advertising, taking clients to lunch, or promotional giveaways. Debtors Anonymous has a special section called Business Owners Debtors Anonymous because business owners can make a case to justify endless expenses because they're "good for business" or "tax deductible." And that can trap them in an endless cycle of overspending.

You have to make sure you're charging enough to meet your income goals.

Entrepreneurs love to get new clients for their businesses. They work hard developing their skills and marketing them and then the payoff comes when someone says, yes, they want to hire them. But you have to make sure you're charging enough to meet your income goals. If you are an entrepreneur or hope to be one, here are some guidelines to ensure that you take everything into consideration when pricing your services:

1. *Calculate your "profit price."* Create a monthly operating budget for your business that factors in all your costs including overhead, sub-contractors, taxes, salaries, marketing expenses, and every variable you can think of. Factor in irregular expenses that occur annually or quarterly, such as insurance expenses, annual tax preparation fees, or Christmas gifts. Don't forget repairs and maintenance and an allowance for refunds or bad debts. Total all these expenses and then add an additional 5 percent for contingencies (because you will have forgotten something!) and an additional percentage for your profit. Now add in your income goal, which would be equal to the salary you would be paid if you were employed by someone else, plus fringe benefits including a retirement plan. Divide this total by the number of hours you want to (or are willing to) work each month and that will tell you the hourly rate you must charge for your service.

Examples:

Expenses	+ 5%	+ 10%	+ Income Goal	= Total	/ Total Hours	= Hourly Fee
$2,000	+ $100	+ $200	+ $3,750	= $ 6,050	/ 130	= $ 46.54
$2,000	+ $100	+ $200	+ $5,000	= $ 7,300	/ 130	= $ 56.15
$3,000	+ $150	+ $300	+ $10,000	= $13,450	/ 130	= $103.46

You might question whether or not this hourly rate is competitive for your type of business. The rule of thumb is to be priced in the "high middle" range of your competition. If your income goal calculation puts your hourly fee too high, then you must trim expenses, work more hours, reduce your income expectation, choose another line of work with a higher profit potential, or get very creative.

2. *Not all work hours are billable hours.* When calculating your "profit price," don't forget that you will work a number of hours "on" your business but not "in" your business. That means that not all of your time is billable to a customer—there is administrative time writing letters, doing budgeting, billing, or accounting, and marketing time making phone calls, going on appointments, attending networking meetings, etc. Entrepreneurs are often overly optimistic about the number of hours each week they can work on client business and perform all these other tasks and therefore overestimate their income potential. Or they find themselves working too many hours each week and then burning out. Make sure to take this into account when figuring your "profit price." Raise your price rather than increase the number of hours you're willing to work or find someone to delegate to.

3. *Marry your "profit price."* That is, be faithful to your income goal and avoid the temptation to lower your fees to your absolute bottom line in order to get business. Yes, you work hard marketing in order to find someone who wants to hire you, and you are anxious to make the deal. But everyone knows cheapest price doesn't equal best quality. You will find that the clients who are shopping for the lowest fees are the most difficult and demanding to work for and you will spend more time than you will be paid for on their work. Stand firm on your "profit price" and you may have fewer clients initially but they will be higher quality clients—Dolphins—easy to work for and

happy to pay you. And it often happens that the higher your fee, the more respect you get.

Sometimes you can eliminate yourself from consideration by a client because your rate is priced too far under market. The prospective client might then assume that you are either new at this, not good enough, or in financial trouble. A friend of mine started a home-based business doing computer consulting. When she called a friend to solicit business and told him her price was $50 per hour, he told her that he could not recommend her unless she charged at least $90 per hour. She understood then that he could only refer his customers to a top-notch professional and that such a professional would charge this kind of fee.

The time and care you invest in pricing your services will pay off handsomely as you start to meet and then exceed your income goals. You are successful and you deserve it!

Think Outside the Safe Deposit Box

Financial Stress Reduction is simply this: earn more money, spend less money, or find a creative way to get what you want.

So far, we've talked about practical strategies for earning more money and budgeting the money we have. But what are some creative ways to get what we want or save money without going through the usual maneuvers? For this, you need imagination. You need to look at the world in a new way.

There's more than one way to protect your assets, save money, or arrange to obtain expensive items that don't fit into your current budget. My fellow coach and seminar leader, Adoley Odunton, told me the story of how she created attending an expensive conference in another state—for free!

A Zillionaire Story: Free Travel and a Free Seminar
"Where there's a will...

"In August 2000, I heard that one of my favorite teachers, Mary Manin Morrissey, was leading a women's conference in Oregon. With airfare, accommodations, and conference fees, I needed $900. There was no way I could afford it. But I had a nagging feeling that it was very important for me to be at that conference. I began doing my affirmations and visualization exercises—seeing myself at the conference having a wonderful time. If I was meant to be there, I knew Spirit would find a way. I called and asked if they had spaces available. Cathy said they had a few left but were selling out fast. I told her that I wasn't able to buy a ticket *yet* but I knew I was supposed to be there so she should reserve a place for me. 'Don't sell my ticket without calling me. I know that ticket's meant for me.' A little amused, she agreed. Each week, I checked in to see if my ticket was still available. The tickets were moving fast but she confirmed it was. A month went by. Instead of manifesting more money, I had more debts.

> **Financial Stress Reduction is simply this: earn more money, spend less money, or find a creative way to get what you want.**

"A month before the conference I received a letter from Delta Airlines telling me that my frequent flyer miles had doubled. I now qualified for a return trip to Portland. A week later I received a call from Fiona whom I had met at a previous conference. She lived in Portland. Was I planning to come to the Women's Retreat? Could she pick me up at the airport and be my wheels during the conference? Now with my transportation covered, I was happily looking forward to the trip.

"My hopes were dashed ten days before the conference when I received a notice that I owed money to the IRS. Then the phone rang. It was Cathy. They were sold out and had three buyers for my ticket. Did I have the money to pay? I looked at the IRS bill in my hand. 'You better sell my ticket.' Maybe what I thought was my intuition was simply wishful thinking.

"Later that evening, as I meditated, I finally decided to let go and let God. I had done all I could. If I was supposed to go, a way would be found. I threw myself into work.

"Three days before the conference, Cathy called. The woman who had bought my ticket had called to say her promotion had finally come through and it was taking her out of town. She was tithing her ticket in gratitude. 'Well, Adoley, you were right. It was your ticket and it's come back to you.' I received a full scholarship to the conference!"

Adoley took action to put herself in the way of receiving this "gift from the Universe." She thought positively and visualized herself at the conference, sent out ships, counted her money, was honorable about her IRS obligation, did her job, prayed for her highest good, and was open to receiving good. The Universe is the quarterback throwing touchdown passes all the time—but it's got to find an open receiver. You can be the receiver—you just have to do the footwork to get yourself into position to catch the pass. Then you can run for the touchdown.

Everyone has talents. Everyone can think positive. Everyone can pick up a telephone. Anyone can write down a goal. Anyone can design a budget. Anyone can help someone else. Most people don't.

Zillionaires do.

Strategy 6 | Your Zillionaire Time Frame Starts Now

"Don't wait to live a Passionate Life until you have all your ducks in a row. Quite frankly, you may never have all your ducks lined up because inevitably one duck will get sick, another duck will have stage fright, one duck may feel ugly that day, one duck may procrastinate, the other duck may feel fat that day, the other duck may be a perfectionist, the other duck may feel upset and unappreciated, the other duck may want to be the center of attention, and YOU will still be an older duck wondering what would it have been like to live a Passionate Life."

—Deborah Deras

It was a Winnie-the-Pooh kind of blustery day, after a rainstorm. The wind darted fitfully through the puddles in the parking lot; sunlight silvered the edges of a few remaining clouds. Gusts blew strands of hair into a nimbus around me as I strolled to my car, the box boy following me with my cart full of groceries.

Filled with that joy of living that sometimes sails on the breeze of such a day, I threw my arms wide and said, "Isn't this a glorious morning?" as I opened the trunk of my car.

The young man smiled as he started loading my trunk with my newly purchased goodies. "I was just thinking of that song," he said, and started singing, "Oh, what a beautiful morning…"

"Oh, what a beautiful day…" I joined in.

He turned to me and we sang the rest of the chorus together in full voice: "I've got a beautiful feeling, everything's going my way!"

Several people walking by looked at us curiously, but we didn't care. We laughed together and I clapped my hands, delighted with this moment of shared connection. "What's your name?" I asked, smiling happily.

"Ken," he replied. "What's yours?"

"Chellie," I said, and extended my hand. He took it and we shook hands. "Pleased to meet you," we said in chorus, and laughed again. We wished each other a beautiful rest-of-the-day and waved goodbye.

No, we're not quitting our day jobs or trying out for *American Idol*. Not every moment has to lead to some big thrilling conclusion or life change. It's just a moment out of time, when the cares and the goals and the worries and the to-do lists fade into inconsequence, and we live truly in the moment of now.

> **Not every moment has to lead to some big thrilling conclusion or life change.**

Eckhart Tolle wrote an entire book called *The Power of Now,* but all you really need to know is what Baba Ram Dass said in the sixties: "Be here now." Pay attention to this precious second of your life. And this one. And this…

When you have "too much on your plate" and you are rushed to get everything done, you are missing your life. Life isn't in the to-do list or the fear of "what will happen if" or the longing of "I'll be happy as soon as." It isn't in your dreams or plans or goals. Life is in the spaces between those things.

When was the last time you sang with the box boy at the market?

Overcoming Overwhelm

This chapter isn't about getting more done, but getting less done. I remember years ago watching Michael in the television series *Thirtysomething* say words to the effect that "all of life boils down to six activities: 1) eating, 2) sleeping, 3) goofing off, 4) work—if you're lucky, 5) sex—if you're really lucky, and 6) looking for a place to park."

I don't think we do enough goofing off.

In the spring of 2005, the non-profit organization Families and Work Institute released a study entitled *Overwork in America*. They found that one-third of the respondents felt chronically overworked, and more than half reported feeling overwhelmed at least once in the past month by the amount of work they had to accomplish. More than half complained that they were often asked to work on too many tasks and were interrupted too many times, and that resulted in difficulty in completing projects. Nine out of ten said that although they worked hard, they didn't have enough time to get everything done. Seventy-nine percent of those surveyed said they had paid vacation time in 2004, but 36 percent weren't planning to use it.

> **This chapter isn't about getting more done, but getting less done.**

And those that do take vacations often take along their cell phones, pagers, laptops, Blackberrys, etc. and keep right on working while the Seine or the Danube or the Mississippi rivers roll on by, ignored and unappreciated. People laugh and say to me, "What's a vacation?" They are so afraid they'll miss a phone call or that they won't get all of their work done that they don't even go out of town. A poll by the National Federation of Independent Business showed that most small businesses are open for eleven hours a day, usually beginning at 8:00 a.m., and more than 25 percent of them are open seven days a week.

Does this sound like you? I told a fellow business owner that I was excited about my upcoming vacation, and she rolled her eyes and said, "What's a vacation? I haven't had a vacation in six years." I was horrified. "You don't get them back, you know," I said. She stared at me. "It isn't like you save them up and some year you get six vacations. Those six vacations are lost forever. If I were you, I'd schedule one helluva grand vacation for myself right away!"

Do you work even when you're sick? Comedienne Rita Rudner says, "I work for myself, which is great. Except when I call in sick—I know I'm lying." The common wisdom about owning your own business is that you can work half-days. And you can choose which half you want to work—the first twelve hours or the second twelve hours.

Are you bragging about how you suffer for your business? Or your art? Or your job? Or your children? You build the mouse trap, you put the cheese in it, you snap it shut on yourself, you whirl on the treadmill, and then you complain about your mousey life. Besides that, you're a cranky little mouse. Do you think you're not wearing that "I'm-so-busy-please-don't-interrupt-me" face? You think I can't hear the annoyance in your voice when I call and I've disturbed you? Who do you think wants to hire cranky, rushed people? And who wants to marry them?

Are you a Zillionaire or a mouse?

Get a Better Job, Get a Better Life

Not only are we working too hard, but a lot of us are working at jobs we don't even like!

I was asked to give a speech to a group of hospital employees, and the woman who had arranged the meeting sent me a copy of the invitation she had mailed out. My eyes widened as I saw that it said I would be giving "special tips on retirement planning." Since I am not a financial planner and don't do retirement planning, I called the woman and asked her what that was about. "Oh, yes," she laughed nervously, "I just know our people are interested in that, so I thought you could say something about that for us."

Swell.

The day of the talk, everything was going smoothly, and people were listening and laughing, when I suddenly remembered I needed to say something about retirement.

"I was asked to give you a tip about retirement planning," I began, and I saw people perk up to listen. "So here's my tip: don't retire."

The audience looked at me quizzically.

"If you are working at a job you hate just to put in enough time to get your pension and retire, you are wasting your life. Did you ever hear of a movie star saying, 'I can't wait until I have my pension funded so I can retire and stop making all these movies'? No. Because actors love their work. At ninety years old, they're trying to convince insurance companies how healthy they are so that they can make a movie. They die onstage. They want to die working because they love their job. **Find work you love and you won't want to retire from it.** Then you can live life richly, fully, enjoying every day, instead of waiting for the day when you can retire. Retire to do what? Lie on the beach? For how many days would that be interesting?

"Besides, a lot of people don't make it to age sixty-five. Many people die before they reach retirement age. So I suggest you don't wait to enjoy life until you retire. Besides, if you live unhappily all your working life, you'll be locked in the habit pattern of living unhappily. Start enjoying life now, or you won't know how to later."

I could see that some of these people weren't that happy about what I was saying. I could tell from looking at them that many of them didn't love their jobs. It showed on their faces. What they really wanted was The Magic Answer of how they could retire quickly—like how they could get a million dollars saved by next week—so they could be free to do what they wanted.

It doesn't work like that. It takes time—unless you win the lotto. But planning to win the lotto isn't a good retirement plan because it only works for one out of twenty million people. Oh, you could be the one! I just suggest you have a back-up plan in place in case it happens a little further down the road than you expect, if someone else is doing more affirmations every day than you are...

Make the Days of Your Life Count

There's an ancient Sufi story of a wealthy man who worked hard all his life amassing a fortune. Growing older, he took a break from work to decide what to do next, and just at that moment, Death came for him. He tried to bargain with Death, offering him one hundred thousand dinars for an extra year of life. Death said no. Two hundred thousand dinars then, the man begged. Death said no. The man scrambled and pleaded, offering half his fortune for one extra hour of life, but Death was implacable. Finally, the man offered his entire fortune for just one extra moment. Death agreed and the man wrote, with his last breath, a message to humanity: "Be careful with your time. I could not buy one additional hour of life for five hundred thousand dinars."

Do you value the hours of your life? Are you working at something you love and believe in and are committed to? Or are you at least working at something that is preparing you for the work you were born to do? Do you hate to wake up in the morning because you hate your job? I had those days once. Days when I woke up in the dark just before the alarm rang, and thought, Oh please, don't be time to get up yet. I don't want to have to go to that job. Those were the worst days of my life.

> **Do you value the hours of your life?**

Don't wait another day to be happy and fulfilled in your work. Get out. Get another job. I don't care how tight the job market is—have you ever seen a newspaper without want ads in it? Read them from the first "A" all the way to the last "Z," even engineering or sales or anything you think isn't your style or your experience or your education. You'll get creative ideas just by looking at them. Call executive search companies, search the Internet, send the word out to your network. Go back to school if you need a degree to do the thing that really interests you, that makes your soul sing.

A psychologist I worked with once told me that she enrolled in graduate school to get her doctorate when she was forty years old. "Why are you doing that?" her friends asked. "You'll be fifty before you get your PhD!" She answered, "I'm going to be fifty anyway. I'll either be fifty without a PhD. or fifty with a PhD. I'd rather be fifty with one." And ten years later, she had her doctorate in psychology. But she was happy every year while she was working on her goal, not just the years since achieving it. The happiness of life is in the *pur-*

suit of happiness. The artist doesn't paint one picture, hang it on the wall, and stare at it for sixty years. The joy of the artist is in the act of creating. And creating. And creating…

The happiness of life is in the *pursuit* of happiness.

If you want to join the hordes of Tuna working their lives away in "quiet desperation," waiting for their Social Security check to give them respite from soul-deadening work, be my guest. But if you want to join the Dolphins who are working toward Zillionaire status, you have different requirements to satisfy. No Zillionaire hates their job.

Social Security was set up in the 1930s with the retirement age set at sixty-five because most people died by age sixty-three. Social Security was never intended to be something that supported everyone for the last twenty-five to thirty years of their lives. It was a stopgap measure to take care of the few people who outlived the norm and were too frail or sick to work. But like most things in our lives, our political habits also outlive the circumstances they were designed to fit. Politicians who serve at the will of the people have a difficult time asking those same people to give up their benefits. It's an unpopular political stand to tinker with Social Security—especially if you want to raise the retirement age—but that is what needs to happen.

You can be angry about that; you can complain that you paid taxes lo these many years and you shouldn't have those benefits you counted on taken away from you, but guess what? Play "show me the money!" and count it up: No government can keep High Budget spending on Low Budget income forever. Some ingrained political habits need to be broken.

But you are a Zillionaire-in-training, so don't wait for the government to catch up. You aren't interested in living your senior years on Social Security Low Budget anyway. You need to take your own actions to make sure you are living life to the fullest and saving pots of money for later, too—but much later. Consider me your habit-breaker, the counter-intuitive financial advisor who says retirement is not the goal. Saving money is not the end-all and be-all of your life. It's just a line item on your budget. It deserves attention and contributions, but not everything. As the Citibank advertisement said, "If you gave up your morning coffee for a year, you could make an extra mortgage payment. But man, you'd be grumpy."

Work Fewer Hours, Make More Money

The secret is that you can make more money if you work less. When you're overwhelmed, you can't be efficient or effective—you usually have trouble just getting started on all the tasks you have to do. When you're overwhelmed, you find yourself pushing too hard and driving too fast, and there's certainly no singing in parking lots.

I'm heartily tired of listening to the endless complaining litanies "I'm too busy," "I'm so overwhelmed," and the new phrase *du jour* "I have too much on my plate." Life is a big smorgasbord, and it is tempting to try to pile it higher and higher

> The secret is that you can make more money if you work less.

with tasty morsels. But half of what you put on your plate isn't nourishing you, but only weighing you down. You end up bloated and uncomfortable, yet you go back for seconds and then dessert. Everything looks so good and you don't want to miss out on anything. Yet your hunger is not appeased; you are still looking for that tasty bite that is perfect.

So people work sixty, seventy, eighty hours a week at their job; meanwhile they have a spouse and three children and a hobby and a spiritual group and a nonprofit fundraiser they volunteered for and friends they have to keep up with and shopping and visiting Grandma in the nursing home and taking out the trash and doing the bank recon-

You can have everything you want, just not all at once.

ciliation and arranging the family vacation and Christmas shopping on the vacation so that's all done before the rush is on and grocery shopping and the favorite television show and cooking and cleaning and...

...And when was I going to write that screenplay? When was I going to learn to fly that plane? Dance the swing? Learn to sing? Play ball with my daughter? Fly a kite with my son?

You can have everything you want, just not all at once. You need to look over the Life Buffet, choose to put a few choice things on your plate and leave the rest for another time. It's time to simplify. Get up from the table before you are overstuffed. If we organize our priorities better, we can scrape a lot of fat and filler off our plates.

A client of mine named Kathy called frantically one day: "Chellie, you've got to help me! I have too much to do and I've got to get some help organizing and managing my time."

When I showed up at her office to help, she was in a sorry state and handed me her six page to-do list. I looked at it briefly and said, "Well, you can't get all this done this week."

She stared at me. "That's not this week's list," she said, "that's *today!*"

I hung my head in my hands with a sigh. No wonder she was so frantic all the time. She was smart and talented and operating on a high wavelength, but it was frazzled. She reminded me of the people on the old *Star Trek* episode where they moved so fast you couldn't see them—you just heard a high-pitched buzzing in your ears as they passed by.

I told her I was sorry to disappoint her, but I hadn't brought my magic wand with me and I couldn't create another thirty-six hours in the day for her to get all her projects done. She had signed up for too many and piled her plate high with obligations. There was nothing to do but scrape half of the stuff on her plate into the garbage pail. She needed to resign from a bunch of projects.

She was horrified when I told her that, of course. "Well, I said I would do these things," she lamented. "I can't just call them up and say I can't get it all done."

Some of your obligations have to go, and it'd be better if you did it now voluntarily instead of later because you were dead from overwork.

"Yes, Kathy, you can," I said. "If you died tonight, guess what? They'd appoint someone else to take your place tomorrow. When a poker player leaves the table, nobody cares where he's going or why. The dealer just hollers, 'Seat open,' and someone else fills the seat. Some of your obligations have to go, and it'd be better if you did it now voluntarily instead of later because you were dead from overwork."

That made an impression. Then we got to work separating out the choice tasty morsels on her plate from the tofu and the peas (or whatever is your least favorite food).

Here's how you do it:

1. Make a list of everything on your plate.
2. Reorganize the list in order of priority.

3. Chop off the bottom third.

4. Call everyone you need to call that's part of the bottom third and resign, cancel, abdicate, cede, quit, withdraw, relinquish, retract, and surrender.

You are not your to-do list. You made up your to-do list. You can opt out of anything on it anytime you choose. The time to choose is now.

Spending the Time of Your Life

Before deciding how you *want* to spend your time, you might like to take a look at how you *are* spending your time. Make a check-list to help figure this out. Be honest—you don't have to show your list to anyone else, so don't fool yourself. You will clearly see the difference between what you think you are committed to having in your life and what you actually spend your time on. There are 168 hours in every week. How many hours are you spending on your number-one priorities? Sending out ships? Eating? Sleeping? Having fun? How many hours do you spend with your spouse? How many hours are you spending on income producing activities? Sales calls? Email?

Look at the truth of your life in this list. Are there things you would like to change? How is the ratio of fun versus work? How many hours are you spending doing income-producing activities? If you own a business and want to double your income, double the time you're spending on doing the things that make money. Are you spending time with your spouse? I read that the average American couple spends approximately five minutes a day talking with each other. That's thirty-five minutes out of 168 hours a week. How can you expect a relationship to last if you only give it that much time and attention? Perhaps you're not married yet, but want to be. Then how much time are you spending dating? Going to singles events? Sending out relation-ships? How about time with your kids? What about that novel you want to write?

Yeah, yeah, I know, it's just that you have so much on your plate…

Let me give you a tip: Break the damn plate and start over from scratch. Grab a new plate, go back to the buffet line, and just pick out the delicacies you really want. Then write out your new list in order of priority. And make sure you give the highest priority items the most amount of time.

When you are committed to a project, you put it at the top of your list. I'll never forget an interview I saw on television with author Toni Morrison. When she was writing her first novel, she was working full-time and raising children. Yet she had a burning desire to write. She said she wrote "at the edges of the day," before the children woke up in the morning and after they went to bed at night. She got her novel published and kept writing. In 1993, she was awarded the Nobel Prize for Literature.

See the difference between what you think you are committed to having in your life and what you actually spend your time on.

We may not all win prizes, but we can all write at the edges of the day if our desire and commitment are strong enough. Look at your Zillionaire goals again. Have you scheduled time for their accomplishment? Have you scheduled time for positive thinking? Are you sending out ships every week? What are you committed to having in your life and how are you backing that up with the commitment of your time?

If you say your number one priority in life is your family, but you're working eighty-hour weeks, you're lying to yourself—and your family. You either need to change your hours, change your job, or own up to the fact that your family is not your number one priority. If you take the time to reflect, you may find you don't want that fast-track at work if it means traveling too many weeks away from your loved ones. You may opt for job-sharing, working part-time, or becoming a stay-at-home parent for a while. You may want to start your own business and keep it small and the hours reasonable. You may find you are happier with more free time to enjoy your family than you are with more money, bigger houses, fancier cars, or gourmet meals.

> **If you say your number one priority in life is your family, but you're working eighty-hour weeks, you're lying to yourself—and your family.**

Do What Makes Money First

If you are in business for yourself, it is easy to let work fill every waking hour of your life. Starting a business involves a huge investment of time in getting all your systems set up, trial and error on what works and what doesn't work to serve your customers, networking, research and development of new ideas, staying abreast of current trends in your industry, etc. The problem is that when you spend so much time in the beginning building your business, working eighty-hour weeks becomes your new habit. That's what your mind begins to tell you is necessary for your business survival. Then fear of financial insecurity runs your business and that's when your business starts running you.

But corporate ladder-climbers often work the same long hours, and so do lots of administrative wage-earners who care about doing a good job. I'm not saying not to give. I'm saying not to over-give. The number of hours you work is not an appropriate measure of your commitment, anyway.

There comes a time when you have to break that habit in order to create more time for your life in your work schedule. If you pay attention to what makes money in your business and spend the majority of your time and energy on those things, you can streamline all your systems so that your business serves your life instead of vice versa. You can convince clients and bosses of this if you gather the proof and then make the sale. That's what I want you to do.

There are three rules for making money in business:

1. Do what makes money now. Can you pick up the phone today, make a call, make a sale, and get money right now? Can you have a discount sale this weekend and have cash that day? Can you work a part-time job and get money in a regular paycheck at the end of the week if you are just getting your business off the ground or sales are slow? You know what your budget is, and you need to do whatever it takes to make money now so you can pay your bills now. You need bread and butter canoes that keep you solvent from day to day.

2. Do what makes money soon. These are marketing activities that don't directly produce income now, but produce contacts that will produce money soon. These are networking activities, newsletters, and emails that are going to produce money eventually, but not necessarily today. If you spend time arranging speaking engagements a couple of months in advance, they will produce "Soon Money" after the speaking event has been held. These are your schooners.

3. Do what makes money later. Some of your bigger sales will take longer to close. Big ships sail slower. If you are selling a 10,000-item order to a department store, the sale will take longer and the money will come in later than if you just sell one item to a customer today. This book is a perfect example of "Later Money." Yes, I got some money as an advance upon signing the contract, but the majority of my money will come later in the form of royalties, which only get paid every six months. This is potentially good money, but I will starve to death at the dock if I ignore the canoes that bring in money today and only focus on the cruise ships that bring in money far off in the future.

But whatever you do, in any case, *do what makes money first!*

It is also important to spend a portion of your time on residual income-producing activities, so that you aren't totally dependent on working each day in order to make money. When I decided to write a book, I had to reorganize my time-priorities list in order to include it. Writing became my fourth priority. I have to keep my main business profitable so that I still make a living while I write my book, but if I don't put writing time in my schedule, there won't be a book. Getting paid for the book is mostly "Later Money," but it also creates an additional income stream that I call "making money while you sleep." When my book is in the bookstores, it is being sold by people all over the world, twenty-four hours a day, even while I am asleep. My books can be producing income for me—and my heirs—for years into the future, long after I am no longer working.

> **But whatever you do, *do what makes money first!***

Actors have known this for years, and that's why they negotiate residual income to be paid to them when their movies are sold in other markets or run on television. But that isn't enough. There is a reason that famous celebrities design clothing lines, or perfumes, or write songs they publish as well as sing. They are creating residual incomes that will last long after their careers have faded—even after their deaths. Elvis Presley and Graceland is a good example of that.

The motion picture industry often makes as much or more money from ancillary products as they do from the movies themselves. You can invest in real estate, stocks, bonds, etc. You can design a web-based business, with products, e-books, and online training courses that people can buy automatically at any time. Then you spend your time marketing to get people to the website. If you join a multi-level sales organization, you can train other people and make a profit from their sales as well as your own.

> **Administrivia is the biggest time waster.**

Every other business activity is administrivia and can be put off, delegated, boiler-plated, streamlined, and otherwise made efficient and fast. Administrivia is the biggest time waster. We want to make our papers perfect, because then we feel like we're doing a good job at our work. But the real reason—the hidden reason—we love to shuffle our papers is because it makes us feel like we are working, when really we are avoiding.

So the way we spend our time actually breaks down like this:

A) Time spent doing things that make money

B) Time spent doing things that cost money

C) Time spent doing things that make you feel like you're working but are really an avoidance of A

What we are avoiding is the real work of the business—no, not the delivery of the product or service: we adore that part! That's what we're in business to do and why we started our business in the first place. There isn't one business owner I know who wouldn't love to have a roster full of clients all ready to pay money for us to do what we love doing. But we won't have them unless we do the most difficult and confrontational part of the business: we have to find prospects and sell them our products or services, which is what turns them into clients. The hard part—the confrontational part—of business is sales. We don't always like that so much. But that's the A work—and that's where the money is. And so that's where your time should be spent.

> **If you are going to hire salespeople, you are responsible for their training, which means that you have to learn how to do it first.**

Let me give you a tip: Entrepreneurs who are reluctant to sell, who hate to get on the phone and "bother" people, are always telling me they'll just hire someone to do the selling for them. I say great, you can certainly do that. But if you want someone good, you will have to train them, and if you don't know how to sell, how are you going to do that? And you will need to pay them extremely well, too. But the entrepreneurs I know usually mean they're going to hire a telemarketer for $10 per hour. Let me share with you what you get for that.

I met Cheryl at a networking group. She taught seminars just like I do. A week after meeting her and exchanging cards, I got a call from her assistant, Candy.

"Hi, this is Cheryl's assistant, Candy," she said breathily when I answered the phone.

"Hi, Candy," I said.

"Cheryl's having a seminar on Saturday," she said.

"Yes," I acknowledged.

"So, are you coming?" Candy asked.

"No," I said.

"Okay, bye," Candy said.

This is not a sales call. There was no inquiry about me or my interests to see if the seminar is appropriate, or if I might be interested later. It didn't move our relationship forward. Actually, it went backward in my estimation. It was too self-serving, too cut-and-dried. If you are going to hire salespeople, you are responsible for their training, which means that you have to learn how to do it first, see?

Schedule Money-Making Time First

The most important thing in making time for sales calls is to schedule that time in your calendar. If you have time blocked off for them in your calendar each week, you will make the calls. If you leave it to chance or when you have a free moment, it always turns out that there are no free moments, you don't make the calls, then there is no business and then you are broke. It's like waiting to save money until the end of the month when there's extra money left over—have you ever had extra money at the end of the month? No, because it's almost the first again when the rent and mortgage and car payment are due…you can see how that works.

So I schedule my workshops, schedule my speaking engagements and networking groups, and then I schedule my calls. I have found that I work best in the mornings and in the evenings, so I network, teach and make calls during those hours. Essentially, I work my own split-shift, taking afternoons off instead of evenings to relax, meditate, watch TV, and nap. I schedule my sales calls for Tuesday, Wednesday, and Thursday mornings. I avoid Mondays, because I have found people are just getting back from the weekend and are trying to get back into their work habits themselves. They typically aren't as open to talking to me then. I don't schedule calls on Fridays because I like to take Fridays off.

Habits either serve you or sink you.

This structure serves me and serves my business. Making calls these same three days during these same hours makes sales calls a habit. Habits either serve you or sink you. The advantage to having a sales habit is that you don't have to think about it any more. I don't have to go through all that mishigas like, "Oh dear, I know should make some sales calls, but I really need to organize my office first" or "I've got to answer all these emails" or "I have to wash my hair." I can't have any of that. If it's Tuesday at nine, it's telephone time. It's my habit. So I pick up the phone and start making calls.

Decide now which days are your best days for making sales calls and what time is your peak energy time, then block off that time in your calendar to do it. Choose the same days every week and you will find after a short time that you have made it a habit—and a discipline that supports you to make more money. Use your Ship's Log to keep you honest, and to give you the data that will tell you if you are making enough calls to make the sales you want to produce the money you want.

Goofing Off to Take a Load Off

A sure sign you've got too much on your plate is when you look at all the piles of work and all the items on your to-do list, your blood pressure is rising, and then you bail out and do silly stuff instead of money stuff.

I must now confess that I am currently failing the time management section of my own workshop. I was tempted to make this chapter just one page that said "Ran out of time to write this one." In addition to all my regular work teaching classes, giving speeches, networking, and making sales calls, I have now added writing a book. I'm sitting in my bulky, white terrycloth bathrobe, hair afrizz, no makeup, writing away, and it's two o'clock in the afternoon. I feel like Michael Douglas in his old pink bathrobe in *Wonder Boys*, sitting with his too-long novel that he can't seem to finish. If you want to really test your time-management skills, sign a contract and get a deadline for writing a book. When I apologize about my hopeless attire to my roommate, she says brightly, "But look at all the time you're saving not getting dressed!" I look at her bleary-eyed across the piles of papers and chapters and bills and Ship's Logs all around me hollering for attention. I am grumpy, and I am not amused that she is playing the Glad Game.

But then she suggests lunch, and food always brightens me up. So I take a break, we eat, and then we change the light bulbs in the hall lamp. And then I check my email and write answers to a bunch of them, keeping in touch with my network, and I read about the new seminar I should go to and learn how to develop products to sell on my website and blogs and e-zines, and viral marketing on the Internet I should have so I can make $50,000 a month and speak at big conferences for big bucks and it's all so overwhelmingly promotional and makes me feel like I can never get everything done that I should be doing and O-God-I-have-an-e-zine-with-thousands-of-subscribers-and-I-haven't-written-a-newsletter-in-three-months-and-I'm-going-to-lose-them-all-if-I-don't and where is my Colonel Parker to manage all this business for me anyway?

I play a game of Freecell. Oh, goodie, then the phone rings and I talk to a buddy. "Saved by the bell" is a reality in my life. Chattering away, I look around at my clutter and the piles of research material and unfinished books I should be reading and this unfinished chapter I should be writing and my deadline is three weeks away and all I really want right now is to go take a nap...

Distractions are always clawing at you to take you off-purpose.

Does any of this sound familiar to you? Not the details of the distractions, but the fact that distractions are always clawing at you to take you off-purpose?

Distractions come for three reasons: 1) to give your mind a creative break from overwhelm; 2) because you have the habit of laziness; and 3) fear about doing what you know you should be doing, but it's difficult or confrontational or both.

Here are the cures:

1. Creative breaks. If you work too long at something without a break, your thinking starts to get old and stale and circular. A good cure is to go for a walk or go for a drive. For some reason, moving helps your mind unpretzel. I never get creative ideas while I am busy in the middle of my to-do list, especially if it has too much on it. Creative ideas come while I am at rest. For this reason, it is important for me to actively plan my schedule with chunks of unallocated time in my calendar. Our minds crave rest just as our bodies crave rest. It's no good complaining about being overwhelmed. The solution is to build underwhelm into our time management systems.

2. The habit of laziness. This is inertia: a body at rest stays at rest, a body in motion stays in motion. It's not lazy to take creative breaks, but if your breaks aren't creative or they take up twenty of the twenty-four hours in your day, you may just be in the habit of never completing projects, never beginning projects, or getting stuck in the "I-don't-know-what-I-want" stage of life—which can last your whole life if you're not careful. Make a goal, make a plan, and put the plan on your calendar. When you are committed to its achievement, you will take the actions and send out the ships to bring home the treasure. Organizing your time with your number-one Zillionaire goals in mind will help you past the habit of laziness. Having somebody give you a "by when?" deadline helps, too.

3. Fear of difficult or confrontational interactions. This is the Big One. This is the problem that keeps many of the people I meet from being successful. The biggest confrontational fear that people have is taking the risk to do something beyond what they already know, like going to a new restaurant, joining a new club, starting a new hobby, or talking to strangers. For employees, this means asking for a raise or a promotion, suggesting a new product line, or advocating a change in systems or procedures at your company. For business owners, this means making phone calls to people they don't know well in the hopes that some of them will become clients or refer them to clients. Everyone's livelihood depends on reaching out to other people, yet this is the scariest and most confrontational thing they could possibly do. And so they don't do it. And so they struggle with money.

Calling Steve Wynn: A Dolphin Becomes a Whale

As I was writing this chapter, I saw how I was delaying making a call of my own for one of my goals. So I geared myself up to make the call.

I warmed up my voice by saying affirmations. I drank some water. I did some physical exercises. Then I laughed at myself for being afraid—what was the worst that could happen? If I made the call, I had a fifty-fifty chance of getting what I wanted. If I didn't make the call, I had a zero chance. Which would you rather have?

So I took a deep breath, put a smile on my face and in my voice, and called Steve Wynn's assistant, Joyce Luman, at the Wynn Hotel in Las Vegas. I introduced myself and explained that I was an author and writing my second book on how to achieve success and happiness. I mentioned that I and two of my friends had a reservation to stay at their hotel in a few days, and that if they had a vacant high-roller suite available, we'd love to stay in it. I would, of course, be delighted to give the Wynn Las Vegas a nice mention in my new book for giving us a free upgrade...

Joyce was lovely and said they only had a couple of the very big four-bedroom suites and they were always occupied with bona-fide "whales," the gaming industry term for mega-buck gamers. (I didn't explain that I am a Dolphin, not a whale.) Joyce let me know that the Tower Suite we had reserved actually were suites that they put their high rollers in. So I was already booked to stay in a high-roller suite without even knowing it! We had a good giggle over that. I told her I'd bring her a copy of *The Wealthy Spirit* when I arrived. Planned to take one to Steve, too, don't you know. It's the first rule of public relations: A-B-P: Always Be Promoting.

The Wynn Hotel was absolutely gorgeous and the Tower Suite spectacular. (Any day that I start by taking a bath in a luxurious oversized tub watching a flat screen bathroom television is a good day. I heartily recommend this experience.) I stopped by the Wynn offices, too, had a lovely meeting with Joyce and gave her my books. Mission accomplished—and another two ships out to sea! That's the beauty of always sending ships—you never know when they might sail back in with a treasure or two in their holds.

One came in fairly soon after that. A month after our visit, I received a big red envelope from the Wynn Hotel. It was an invitation to their inaugural Wynn Las Vegas Signature Slot Tournament with a $30,000 grand prize. The entry was free and came with three complimentary nights in a resort room. I didn't know if it was a coincidence or not, but I sent a nice thank-you note to Joyce!

> So what big ships are sitting in dry dock at your harbor, waiting for you to get up the nerve to send them out? What can you lose? How much can you gain?

So what big ships are sitting in dry dock at your harbor, waiting for you to get up the nerve to send them out? What can you lose? How much can you gain? Make the call. Go for it! Or "I wonder what would have happened if…" will be running through your brain forever.

Dolphins have the discipline necessary to keep sending out ships. Artist Al Hirschfeld once said, "Everybody is creative and everybody is talented. I just don't think everybody is disciplined. That's a rare commodity." Discipline is the habit of doing the things you must do in order to successfully achieve your goals. In the dictionary it is defined as "training that develops self-control, efficiency." Employees must have the discipline to follow the rules set for them by their employers. Business owners must have the discipline to set some rules for themselves and then follow them, which is quite a trick, since one of the hallmarks of being an entrepreneur is an aversion to rules.

Discipline is what keeps you suiting up and showing up, even when you don't feel like it. It's only difficult in the beginning before you've made it a habit. Once the habit kicks in, it will feel normal—you'll feel something's wrong if you don't do it. Just review your habits periodically to see that they are still producing the results you want. You have to adjust them from time to time to keep up with the changing world.

The old saying "time is money" is a lie.

So distractions come and I want to flee, but I don't leave my office. Distraction will not win. Discipline and determination to achieve my goals will. I will take my breaks for an hour or so, but then I get back to work.

Time Isn't Money if You Structure It Right

The old saying "time is money" is a lie. When I speak to groups, I ask everyone how many hours they have in a day. After laughing about how many hours they would *like* to have in a day, they all eventually agree: we only have twenty-four hours. All of us, every one of us—from Bill Gates to Donald Trump to Steven Spielberg to you and me and the pizza-delivery person—each get twenty-four hours. But we aren't all making the same money. So working more hours isn't the answer to making more money—at some point we all run out of hours.

When I worked for Edgar Scherick in the motion picture industry, he hired a woman named Caroline to run the television department. Film industry people are notorious for working long hours, so I noticed with interest that Caroline always left the office precisely at six o'clock.

One day as she was leaving, I asked her, "How is it that you are always able to leave the office on time each day, when everyone else seems to work day and night?"

She smiled and replied, "I was trained at X-Y-Z television. The culture there was very different from most show business companies where everyone works so many hours into the night. At X-Y-Z, if you stayed late, it was thought that you must be too stupid to get all your work done in eight hours. So I developed the habit of working efficiently and leaving at six every night."

I loved that. If we leverage our hours more efficiently, we can make more money in less time. Our job is to figure out where the money is and spend the majority of our work time doing that. We can delegate the other tasks to someone else.

If you are an employee, you need to notice which jobs at your company produce money for the company and which jobs involve supporting others who produce money. If you are producing money and can prove your case, you can make another big sale—the sale to your company management for more money for you. Good salespeople can negotiate great salaries, commissions, perks, benefits, travel allowances, and additional time off, too. I worked for an employment agency whose president used to tell the salespeople, "If you can bill twenty thousand dollars per month only working one hour a day, that's fine with me. I'm not going to say anything to you about your hours. But if you aren't billing twenty thousand dollars per month, I want to see you at your desk at nine o'clock."

If we leverage our hours more efficiently, we can make more money in less time.

Focus on results instead of the number of hours it might take to produce the results. Time won't produce results. Effective use of time produces results. Unless, of course, you've agreed to be paid by the hour for your work, in which case you have chained yourself to a system that requires you to put in time in order to get money. If you want to make substantially more money, you have to unchain yourself from the time clock.

Are You Running Your Life or Is It Running You?

The ceaseless bombardment of advertising sometimes gets to me. How do I let the "organ" enlargement people know that I don't possess one of those, so please stop emailing me? That I love all my friends' newsletters, but reading them weekly is too much? I'm hooked on *Days of Our Lives,* but I can't keep up with all the relationships anymore. And the TV commercial breaks annoy me—how do I let them know I have enough stuff?

I want fewer responsibilities, fewer items on my to-do list, less effort. I want more time, more freedom, more daily enjoyment, more peace. I want to run my life, not have it run me. So I say no to some bookings, I don't send out some ships, I skip a couple of networking meetings, I play hooky, and I play poker. When someone asks me on what schedule my newsletter comes out, I say, "The Whenever-I-Feel-Like-It Schedule." The last thing I need in my life is another deadline.

> **Focus on results instead of the number of hours it might take to produce the results.**

Some gals from Orange County called me and asked if I would come down there for eight weeks to give my workshop. I said no thanks. They were shocked. "But you can make money," they said. "There are a bunch of people down here who would sign up!"

"You just want me to come down there so you don't have to do the drive up here to Los Angeles," I replied. Well, yes, they admitted. "But I don't want to do the drive either," I said, "and I don't have to, so I'm not going to. There are about nine million people up here and I only need twelve people, so I'm not going to run out of prospects anytime soon. Anyone who wants what I have badly enough has to drive to me."

I win. They both came to Los Angeles and took the course.

This is another time management lesson I learned the hard way. I ran a course once in a different location. It took me half an hour to pack up, an hour and a half to drive there, and a half hour to set up. Then I taught the class for two and a half hours, packed up and drove home. Total time: six and a half hours. When I teach my class at my house, I put the coffee on, people show up, I teach them, they go home, I turn the coffee off. Total time: three hours. Plus, I like my commute: fifteen steps.

I can't be all things to all people.

I know that I can't be all things to all people. I can't speak at every conference, visit every bookstore, or attend every networking group. At some point, I have to stop and say, that's enough. Enough marketing, enough promotion, enough phone calls, enough radio shows. I don't want to fight the hungry hordes jumping up and down, screaming for fame, "Me! Me! Pick me!" So I don't jump up and down anymore. I'm attracting rather than promoting. People can find me, like the Orange County gals did. If they find my work and appreciate it, I'll be there for them. Otherwise, I am happy and content being here for you.

I've done my work, it's out in the world, and seekers are finding it. One by one, ten by ten, my books are being sold all over the world. My workshops are filling up with participants like Rolf, who sat next to a friend who was reading my book on a plane flight. He gave her his phone number to give to me. I called him, and he and his wife,

Nora, enrolled in my class. I trust the process, I trust life, I trust you. Those who have ears will hear.

Meanwhile, my vacation is coming up, and I always look forward to that. Last year, I took a paddle-wheeler riverboat up the Mississippi from New Orleans to Memphis. I sat back and drank iced tea with my girlfriends and watched the lazy river go rolling by. There was a lot of napping and a lot of great food. Ahhh. This year, my whole family—thirteen of us—is going to Hawaii for sun and fun and food and lying around in a beautiful setting. Every year, I take time to opt out of human doing and recover human being.

It's a Zillionaire's Life. I have it because I chose it. I created it to suit me and it does.

How's yours?

Having the Zillionaire Time of Your Life

You have to decide what commitments of your time and energy work for you. Here's your test: Are you enjoying your life, or are you complaining about it? Do your commitments give you joy? Do you feel alive and energized, or worn out and used up? Are you smiling or are you grumpy?

In his book *The Tipping Point*, Malcolm Gladwell told of John Darley and Daniel Batson's psychological study inspired by the biblical story of the Good Samaritan who stopped to help the traveler who had been beaten and robbed. They asked a group of seminarians to prepare a talk on a biblical theme that was to be given at a building a few blocks away. They told some of them that they had plenty of time to make it to their destination, and others that they were late. Then, on the road between buildings, they placed a man who was slumped over and groaning, and waited to see who would stop to help. Sixty-three percent of the seminarians who had a few minutes to spare before their talk stopped to help, but only 10 percent of those who thought that they were late. Even when the subject of their talk was the Good Samaritan!

Being in a rush, being overcommitted, can take a toll on your life in ways you don't even notice. It can change an otherwise calm and friendly person into someone uncaring of the people around them, unseeing of the circumstances in front of them, and unconsciously controlled by the future they are trying to avoid, instead of truly living and experiencing their present.

I heard a very different story at a group I visited one morning for breakfast. Lily, a very energetic woman, told the story of how she trained with her friend Bill to run the Los Angeles Marathon. When race day came, she ran the strongest, fastest race she could, pushing past her limits, looking often at her watch, caring about every minute shaved from her time. Each minute counted so much to her, because she was striving for her personal best.

You have to decide what commitments of your time and energy work for you.

But as she ran, she kept seeing Bill, who had friends and supporters at various way stations along the road. When he saw his friends hailing him with orange juice and champagne, smiling in the sunlight and cheering him on, he would stop for a few minutes and chat with them and drink their champagne. Then he would resume the race.

Lily ran her best time. Bill had the best time. Which do you want? Is it about the number of minutes or the joy of the race? Does anyone really care how many minutes it took you?

Take another look at your list of how you spend your time. Then revise. Then edit. Then revise again and again, until you like the end product: Zillionaire You.

Strategy 7 | Survive the Storms When Your Ships Are Sinking

Dear Family,
I am in the nurse's office right now. I am crying. Last night I cried all night. We went on a hike and slept over there outside. When I am alone and I have nothing to do I always get home-sick. At night I always get sick but otherwize I am having fun. Please mommy and Carole meet me at the bus. This has been a rather sad letter but that is all the news I have for today, and I am sorry. Goodbye, Love, Janie
—Letter from summer camp written by my sister, Jane, when she was eight years old

Oh, how our sailor lives are filled with stormy seas! And they begin early, even before the perils of summer camp and being away from home for the first time. Our first breath is a cry, as that mean old doctor swats us on the bottom. Eventually we discover that the doctor was our friend, who gave us our first kick in the hindquarters to help us howl the mucus from our lungs. We don't understand that at the time, of course. We are just indignant at our rough treatment. But human beings learn recovery early. My sister got over her homesickness—she went back to summer camp three times.

What looks like bad news isn't always bad news. The guy who looks like the bad guy isn't always a bad guy. Sometimes he's a good guy in disguise. It takes time to sort this out, to understand the dif-

What looks like bad news isn't always bad news.

ference between a true disaster and none-too-gentle guidance toward the realization of our highest good. I always seem to notice when disaster strikes "out of the blue"—unfair! unfair!—that it really wasn't a complete surprise and there were plenty of warning buoys in the water. I just ignored the "red sky at morning—sailors take warning," the mutinous mutterings amongst the crew, and the mold in the hold. Like Homer in *The Simpsons*, I paddled my canoe past my orange-vested friends' flashlights directing me towards the calm waters, sunny skies, and rainbows, instead choosing to shoot the rapids where thunderclouds loomed and lightning flashed, "Warning! Danger!"

Life's Lemons Lead to Lemon Meringue Pie

White-faced and trembling, my office manager, Carla, handed me the message that would change my life. Just looking at her, my heart sank. I knew something was terribly wrong. What tragedy had struck that made her look so forlorn?

After building my business management firm over four years from one employee and $80,000 annual sales to thirteen employees and $420,000 annual sales, I was flying high. I had just bought out my partners and was going it alone as an entrepreneur. I was on top of the world. Now, horrified and dumbstruck, I read the message Carla handed me and saw my dreams crumble into dust. Our biggest client had just cancelled our contract and was leaving with only two weeks notice. $300,000 a year had just walked out our door—75 percent of my income.

What was I going to do? I wished I had never gotten up that morning. I wished I were dead. I wished the client were dead, too. (So much for positive thinking.) How could they do this to me? How could they reward my hard work and loyalty with such a stab in the back? I considered my options: murder, suicide, bankruptcy. None of them looked attractive.

I mourned for days. Told all my friends my sad story. Wallowed in my pain like the Tuna I was. Told myself how unfair it all was, how awful the client was, and how virtuous and blameless I was. But there were warning signs I had ignored. Some of the members of the client group had groused about our billings. A new president and a new board of directors were taking over the reins of the organization. An important meeting was held without me. The skies had darkened and the waves were rising, but I didn't reduce sail or batten the hatches. So I switched targets and started beating *myself* up instead of mentally pummeling my soon-to-be-ex clients. How could I not have known the client was unhappy? Why wasn't I smarter, more mature, aware, convincing?

> It takes time to understand the difference between a true disaster and none-too-gentle guidance toward the realization of our highest good.

Then the still, small voice inside me, said, "This is all very well, but crying isn't going to get you where you want to go." I sat up when I heard it. I recognized that voice. My Intuition, Guardian Angel, Higher Self, the Voice of Inner Wisdom—call it what you will. But like E.F. Hutton, when that voice speaks, I listen. And in that moment, I saw that I wasn't doomed and I wasn't dead. Like a poker player with only "a chip and a chair" remaining between winning the tournament and elimination, my determination to succeed took over in that moment. I didn't have much left, but I wasn't completely broke yet. I had some chips and I had an office chair. My business might be smaller, but it was still a business. I had built it up once, and I would just have to do it all over again.

> **What looked like the biggest loss of my life was actually the biggest gift.**

Over the next year, I faced huge hurdles and had to negotiate ways over or around them. I had to become very creative in order to survive and enlisted the aid of everyone I knew—family, friends, employees, my banker, my landlords, my clients who stuck with me, and all the vendors I couldn't pay in full each month. I negotiated for smaller office space and lower monthly payments on loans. I sold off equipment and furniture. I haunted networking groups, looking for referrals and new clients. Every day I listened to Robert Schuller's audio tape *Tough Times Never Last—Tough People Do* about people overcoming tragedies—and said to myself, if they can do it, I can, too. I posted a sign that read "EGBOK" (Everything's Gonna Be OK) over my desk, and then got busy. I learned how to make more money, to keep a light touch, to give to others even when I didn't think I had anything to give. And in the process, I grew spiritually, too, finding a new strength, serenity, stability, and self-esteem.

I was going to need that. They say, "It never rains, but it pours." With all the stress I was enduring with my business problems, lessons in "What Really Matters" were delivered six months later. Suddenly, with no warning, my mother died of a heart attack in the middle of the night on Memorial Day. Then, in August, my uncle died, followed by my aunt in November. My cousin's six-month-old baby was diagnosed with incurable cancer in December and died two weeks later. The day after the funeral, one of my best friends called to say her breast cancer had metastasized into bone cancer and she was dying. Two of my clients passed away in the next two months. So many loved ones left me! I cried every day. And I learned the lesson that love is all there is.

This was also the year, 1989, that the recession hit California full-force. The economy spiraled downward and everyone was suffering. Many people had heard my story, that I had weathered a huge crisis in my business and personal life, and asked me to meet with them to tell them how I did it. How was I able to survive? How was I able to keep smiling while I struggled? What were the financial techniques I used to cut my budget and then expand again as business grew? How did I combine a wealthy material life with a wealthy spiritual life? I started counseling clients over lunch. And then I started putting material together for a seminar, and my new career teaching the Financial Stress Reduction workshop was born.

It's been years since that awful day when I thought my life was over. But it had actually just begun. What looked like the biggest loss of my life was actually the biggest gift. What looked like bad news was really good news in disguise. The door that closed was just guiding me to a bigger door, a better door, a richer door. Now I thank God that client left me! Without their lemons, I might never have learned to bake lemon meringue pie.

If you aren't winning enough in your life, it's because you aren't losing enough.

Winning More Requires Losing More

If you aren't winning enough in your life, it's because you aren't losing enough.

What?! you may be thinking. I'm losing plenty, thanks. That can't be right.

It is right. You have to take risks to win. And you don't win every time you take a risk. Success is a percentage game—and it's not even a big percentage. The difference between successful people and unsuccessful people is that successful people are willing to fail more often than unsuccessful people. They are willing to hear "no" and get rejected. Millionaire baseball players bat .300—that means they only hit three balls out of ten. But they make millions because most people can't even hit that many.

Success is a percentage game.

The difference is that winners have an intense, laser-focused attention on the goal—and on winning the goal. They don't see the goal as out of reach; they believe that they will attain it if they just do the right things. If they don't know exactly what the right things are, they are willing to experiment; pay for lessons, workshops, and coaches; and try different things until they happen upon the things that work. Then they do those things over and over and over, ad infinitum, until the goal is achieved. They send out a ship, and then they send out another one. And another one. And another and another and another. It doesn't matter how many ships sink, how many people say no to you; it only matters how many people say yes. So keep on going until enough people say yes. You have to have this kind of determination not to quit and to keep going until the yeses arrive like the next ship on the next wave. Or the one after that.

It's fun to see the goal and see yourself reaching it. That vision is what keeps you going when your ships encounter stormy seas. Sailors learn to sail when they're out on the ocean, not when they're home safe at the dock. What good is the finest navigation equipment, the latest in ship-to-shore radios, new white canvas sails, and scrumptious food stored in the galley if you don't brave the waves?

Yes, it's hard—so what? It's hard for everyone.

Yes, it's hard—so what? It's hard for everyone. If you have another excuse, go back to chapter one and let me kick you in your "but" again. Or you can spend your life commiserating with the other Angry Tuna over how life is too hard.

After my first book was published, I received a letter from a friend congratulating me. She said that she had always had a secret desire to be a writer and had even written a magazine article once. Eagerly, she sent it to the editor of a magazine and waited anxiously for her ship to come in. But this one floundered on the rocks. The only driftwood from the wreckage was a rejection slip. She never tried again.

That's the saddest thing to me—that you are talented, glorious, special, and the world needs you, but you don't trust it. You have had one shipwreck and you are afraid to brave the storms at sea again. One idiot out there—who isn't even Your People—says something mean and you give up your greatness in subservience to their opinion? Stop that! Don't give up the ship! Try again. Build another ship, build another *fleet* if you have to. The only failure is failing to begin again. Your People are out there waiting for you, praying for you to show up. The world needs you, or you wouldn't be here. The only thing stopping you is you. And *that* you can change.

So how do you remain undefeated in the face of lost ships? How do you garner the strength—mental, physical, and spiritual—to build another? And the one after that? How do you face mounting losses, over and over again?

The Five-Step Breakdown-to-Breakthrough Recovery Program

Breakthrough is usually preceded by breakdown. We are usually hanging on to what is in our way, so it has to completely break down before we're willing to let go of it and move on to our greater good. Breakdowns, like breakups, are painful. Here's the 5-Step program to help you recover:

1. Cry. Sometimes there's just nothing so satisfying as a good crying jag. I climb in my bed and weep and wail. Did you know tears release toxins from your body? And blowing your nose does, too, so crying is a healthy, beneficial release.

2. Eat. After crying, I usually have a headache, and I need comfort. I eat the most satisfying junky comfort food I can get while still in my bed cocoon. I want to be bad. Last time, I ate doughnuts and potato chips. Sugar alternating with salt usually does the trick. (This is not a dietary recommendation for more than a day.)

3. Call friends. I need "oh, poor things" and I need my confidence rebuilt. After a recent hurt-feeling crying jag, my friend Michelle whipped me back into shape with this: "You need to be giving headaches, not getting them!" Oh, *yeah*. Thank you!

4. Laugh. I almost skipped this step, moving straight to "Once more dear friends, into the breach!" I know that's Shakespeare and went online to find the right play (*Henry IV*) to quote. The search engine asked: "Did you mean 'Once more dear friends, into the *beach*'?" Hee. Go to the beach—that's a great recovery idea, too.

5. Get back to work. Crying is healing for an hour or an afternoon or a day. Any longer than that, and you've developed a Tuna habit.

This is the Cry-Eat-Call-Laugh-Work program. That's recovery in a nutshell. And it's the last step that's the most important in being a Zillionaire. To implement Step 5, you have to have a goal that matters to you. You have to want it, and you have to want it bad. Lots of people get stuck somewhere in the first three steps, but steps four and five are the most important.

When Thomas Edison was inventing the electric light bulb, it took him some ten thousand experiments to get it to work. But he knew that it was just a matter of time before he tried the right element and he was successful in his quest. He had a single-minded devotion to purpose. His attitude was not that he had had ten thousand failures, but that he had successfully discovered ten thousand things that didn't work. And each element he eliminated brought him closer to his goal of finding the one that did work.

> **We are usually hanging on to what is in our way, so it has to completely break down before we're willing to let go of it.**

This is a popular example of perseverance, but it wasn't the end of the story. Once he had the light bulb working, he had to invent and build the hydraulics and dynamos that created the electricity. He had to figure out how to wire a building and bring the electricity to the bulbs. Meanwhile, the world was being lit by gas lamps. Do you think the people who made the lamps or piped the gas were thrilled about being put out of business by electricity? No one believed in his crackpot idea anyway. He had to *pay* a man in New York City to allow him to wire his building with electricity.

Of course, on the day he threw the switch and lit up that building like a Christmas tree on a dark night, everyone who saw it became quite interested in investing in his new company, General Electric. It's only worth about $130 billion now.

Missed Opportunities Are Like Missed Buses— There'll Be Another One in Five Minutes

Even our friend Thomas Edison wasn't right about everything. He also invented the phonograph. Of that invention, he said, "The phonograph is of no commercial value." Given the billions of dollars generated in the music industry now, I bet he's rockin' and rollin' in his grave over that mistake.

Here's another missed investment opportunity:

Walt Disney was passionate about his goal of creating Disneyland. Big dreams require big money, and he was looking for investors in his company. One potential investor's account told of how Walt took him out to the site in Anaheim where Disneyland was just beginning to be built. As the tractors rolled and dirt was dug, Walt spoke of his vision of the park. He described the different sections: Main Street with horse-drawn carriages, Tomorrowland with its rocket to the moon, Adventureland with a shooting gallery and Golden Horseshoe Revue, Fantasyland with Sleeping Beauty's castle. The investor thought it all sounded too risky. He passed. He didn't invest in Disneyland. He kept his ships safe at the dock.

Later, when Disneyland became a smashing success, the investor calculated that every step he had taken that day back to his waiting car had cost him a million dollars.

People are wrong all the time. The soap opera *Santa Barbara* deemed Julia Roberts "dull." Sharon Stone was rejected by *General Hospital*, and *As the World Turns* nixed Hugh Grant. Mike Medavoy, one of Hollywood's super agents, told a young Steven Spielberg his career was "doomed" and passed him off to another agent. Cary Grant and Jeanette MacDonald did a screen test for Fox but were turned down with this explanation: "We feel neither of these people has a screen personality."

After Sony's Columbia Records label cancelled her, Alicia Keys sold 5.5 million copies of her next album for their competitor and won five Grammys. Ashanti was fired by Epic Records and came back to sell 3.3 million copies of her debut album for a rival. Alanis Morrisette was turned down by record company after record company, until Maverick took her on and her debut album *Jagged Little Pill* sold over 30 million copies worldwide. Bonnie Raitt shot to the top of the charts with two back-to-back albums on Capitol Records that spawned hit singles and won three Grammys apiece—right after her prior record company fired her.

> Losing fires up winners. Their response when someone tells them they aren't good enough, they can't do it, or they're a loser is, "Oh yeah? Watch this!"

Losing fires up winners. Their response when someone tells them they aren't good enough, they can't do it, or they're a loser is, "Oh yeah? Watch this!" They use the rejection as an energetic launching pad to redouble their efforts, sharpen their creativity, and prove the naysayers wrong.

So how many times have you tried to achieve your goal? Who among the people you know have tried something 9,999 times without getting results and still kept on trying? What does it take to keep on keeping on? How strong is your vision? How strong is your belief in yourself?

It is, in the end, a self-esteem issue. You have to believe in yourself when no one else does. You have to believe in yourself, or no one else is going to. It helps to bolster your belief when you have a lot of Dolphins swimming in your pod—Dolphins who will sing to you, "You can do it! You can do anything you put your mind to! We love you! We believe in you!" But then it's up to you to believe what they are telling you. If your pod thinks you are fabulous, you are. If your pod thinks you should go for it, you should. If your pod is full of naysayers, look for a new pod.

And if you have no one else, you have me. I am telling you that you can do it! You wouldn't have gotten this far in reading this book if that weren't true. Are you ready to believe? If you are, then you have to do what I've told you—every step I've written here in this book. If you've forgotten some steps, go back to the beginning and start over. There is always another chance for you, just as often as there is another day.

Let me give you a tip: pay attention along the way. The goal you're here to get might not be the goal you think you're here to get. I set out to be an actor but turned left and ended up a speaker and author. Christopher Columbus headed for the West Indies in the right direction—he just didn't know there was a New World in between.

Be passionate, follow your North Star, and the worst that can happen is you live a life full of great adventures. It's all good.

The Answer to Life's Problems: Duct Tape and WD-40

Someone shared with me that "All of life's problems can be solved with two things—duct tape and WD-40. If it moves and it shouldn't, you need duct tape. And if it doesn't move and it should, you need WD-40." That's a great image for life. You need duct tape to keep you on purpose: to stick to your guns, stick to your ideals, stick to your goals. You need WD-40 to get you up and moving: to get out of bed in the morning, get you to the gym, get you "out of the box."

Distinguishing when you need to use duct tape and when you need to use WD-40 is the tricky part. Many businesses have failed because they didn't see a new product or technology on the rise and stuck to the old way of doing things, playing it safe. Just like food kept in the refrigerator long past its expiration date, sometimes people stay in jobs, neighborhoods, or relationships beyond their fruitfulness. When the ship is sinking, it's appropriate to "jump ship!" You don't have to go down with it.

> Just like food kept in the refrigerator long past its expiration date, sometimes people stay in jobs, neighborhoods, or relationships beyond their fruitfulness.

Then again, it's sometimes best to use that duct tape and stay the course—you don't want to give up on your dream just before it's fulfilled. Maybe the next ship you send out is the one that will bring home the treasure, so you have to know when to heed the cry: "Don't give up the ship!"

The creator of the photocopier machine took his new invention to Kodak first. The copier is a kind of camera, so it seemed a natural connection. However, the Kodak executives rejected it—after all, they had better quality photographic equipment already. They just didn't see the business application of the invention. So the inventor went to Xerox and that's why we Xerox documents rather than Kodak them. The Kodak executives had too much duct tape holding them to their known business model—they needed a squirt or two of WD-40 to rouse them to act on a new idea. The inventor had plenty of WD-40, which helped him create a new business machine, and enough duct tape to refuse to give up in the face of rejection.

How do you know "when to hold 'em and when to fold 'em," to use the famous poker analogy? You use the duct tape and stick to your goals as long as you passionately believe in them and are committed to making them happen. When you enjoy the pursuit of the dream, whether or not it is realized. When your intuition tells you to keep going. And most of all, when you know that you will succeed because you're willing to do whatever it takes to make it happen.

Behind every "overnight sensation" there were years of study, failed attempts, more learning, small successes, and dogged persistence. Lots of duct tape. It looks messy, like a first-grader's taped-together construction paper project. Succeed or fail, your passion and commitment to your purpose will be the WD-40 that moves and inspires you to get up each day, excited about the new possibilities today will bring. If you enjoy your dream and all the steps along the way, you'll be a success every day of your life.

"Freaking Out" Is a Habit

Jenny, a bright and energetic producer/director, emailed me in panic mode: "Do you have a minute to talk? I am stalled again, and I'm freaking! Am I ever gonna figure this stuff out?"

I had been getting a bunch of freak-out calls that month—perhaps it was because Mercury and Mars were both in retrograde at the same time. There's only one answer: don't panic. Freaking out won't get you anything you want.

Freaking out is a *habit*. It feels comfortable because it is a *habit*. You are a freak-out junkie because it's a *habit*.

I know life gets tough sometimes. It's hard to keep the faith, keep thinking positive, and keep sending out ships when storms are blowing and it seems every ship sinks just outside the harbor. But that is all there is. There is no Magic Answer but that one. It is only your will and determination to succeed that will keep you going. You don't try things to see if they will work out—you determine what you want and you dedicate yourself to doing whatever it takes to make it work out. To say, "I'll give this six months and see what happens" is not a mind-set that works. When you do that, the Universe stops working on your behalf and just sits down with you and says, "Okay, let's see what happens." Then the two of you sit there on the dock watching everyone else's ships come in.

> **It is only your will and determination to succeed that will keep you going.**

And no ships come in for you, because when your *now* is full of *freaking out*, what do you think you are going to get on the next wave?

Relax. God has a plan and you're in it. Trust. Do what you're supposed to do and expect your good.

If you need better skills in your chosen profession, take classes, read books, get a mentor or partner in the business who knows more than you. If you don't have enough clients, join a networking group, chamber of commerce, or start cold calling (oops, I mean *gold* calling) from the telephone book. People are always asking me, "How many meetings should I go to?" or "How many calls do I have to make?" My answer is: "As many as it takes to get the number of clients you want!" I make seventy-five phone calls a week for approximately six weeks prior to my workshop, and have about thirty-five to forty enrollment conversations per week. Not all the calls are to different people; sometimes they are second, third, or tenth calls to one person. I call all the people who expressed an interest in my work when I met them—at a networking group, at a party, on jury duty, in line at the post office, etc. (See Chapter 3 for details on sending out ships.) I keep a Ship's Log of statistics on my phone calls, so I know that's what it takes to get my workshop filled.

Then I decided to write a book. It took me six months to get an agent and a year and a half to get a publisher. I didn't count the number of rejections. It didn't matter. I was looking for the yes, and I wasn't going to stop until I got it. Whatever stood between me and that yes was of no consequence. My attitude was determined, rock solid, invincible. Recall when you have been that resolute and unwavering in your determination to have something or to be something, and use it for the things you want now. Wear that thinking—it's the face of success.

> **I was looking for the yes, and I wasn't going to stop until I got it. Whatever stood between me and that yes was of no consequence.**

Your fame and fortune is out there waiting for you, but you have to go get it.

Affirmations work. The hardest time to do them is when you most need to do them. And you have to act your way into feeling happy and rich while you're doing them. Your subconscious mind can't tell the difference between the truth and a lie. Eventually, what you tell it actually becomes true. But you can't do affirmations for five minutes, then freak out for the other twenty-three hours and fifty-five minutes, and expect "feeling groovy" to magically descend upon you. Abraham-Hicks said, "The Universe is responding to you in your *now*. So whatever you're feeling right *now* means that is what you are sending out vibrationally right *now*, which means that is what you are attracting to yourself right *now*, which means your future is *full* of a bunch of stuff that is gonna feel pretty much like right *now* feels." You have to stop feeling the panic, as cushy and fine as it might feel to be a blameless victim of circumstance. Take responsibility. Picture what you want and feel good about already having it. That's faith and belief in action. What you want shows up after that, not before.

Your fame and fortune is out there waiting for you, but you have to go get it.

So I called Jenny, and after about sixty seconds of sympathy, I asked, "How many phone calls did you make last week?"

She hemmed and hawed and talked about emails.

I said, "How many phone calls?"

"Um, three," she answered.

"I'm going to hang up now," I said gently. "Call me back when you've made fifty."

And how many have you made? Enough? Put this book down for an hour and get busy. Send out some ships!

Does Success Make You Nervous?

Fear of failure makes people nervous until they become successful. Then success makes them nervous. When nervousness is a habit, you just choose different things to be nervous about. My friend Sossi Crilly had gotten a new job in the title insurance industry. She wrote me that in her first month, she wrote fifteen orders. The second month she wrote thirty-five, and in the following months forty-two, fifty, and forty orders. A great success!

But success made her nervous. Now that she didn't have to worry about whether she could do it or not, she turned to worrying about whether she could *continue* to do it. You see the problem? If we are in the habit of worrying, there will be nothing safe enough that we can't worry that it will fall apart and destroy us.

> If we are in the habit of worrying, there will be nothing safe enough that we can't worry that it will fall apart and destroy us.

Sossi worked on base plus commission, and in order for her commissions to kick in, she had to close over $10,000. She was closing $16,000 already, so everything was great. But she wrote me that she still had "the fears of getting stranded…blah, blah, blah." She laughed via email when she said she realized the voice she was hearing in her head was her mom's "you'll-never-amount-to-anything" voice. She said, "Sometimes I feel guilty that I am not working as hard as I should be, and don't know how I am getting the orders, instead of patting myself on the back that I am a precious person who is seizing my opportunities and have a vision." She said she wanted me to know that she was going to turn this around. "I am going to San Francisco to visit my daughter and *I am going to enjoy myself.*"

I wrote her back a happy note of congratulations and let her know that the fearful voice thing is in everybody, not just her. I confessed that I have it, too. Sometimes I am amazed that I keep enrolling people in my workshop for so much money. How do I do that, I wonder? And the little doubt creeps in that my house of cards could come crashing down, that I've already enrolled everyone who could possibly want to enroll, that T. Harv Eker is going to get everyone and there will be no one left for me. And why didn't I buy real estate, everyone else got rich in the housing market and I didn't, yada, yada, yada.

Sound familiar? If you're waiting for that voice to disappear, it ain't gonna happen. That's what human beings do. It isn't just you; it's the way our minds operate. What I have changed is I don't wallow in it anymore—that's Tuna behavior. I have developed the practice of turning that voice off within minutes of hearing it, and reaffirming how glorious and wonderful I am! I go read my fan letters, focus on helping others the best way I can, thank God for my wonderful life, smile, and reach out in love.

> **You only take positive action when you focus your thinking on positive future outcomes rather than present challenges and failures.**

Play the Zillionaire Glad Game

Playing the Glad Game helps. I learned this game from the old Disney movie, *Pollyanna*, where the young Haley Mills always looks on the bright side of everything, no matter what tragedy has befallen her. My mom reinforced this with all the family as I was growing up. When something bad happened, we could cry and feel badly about it for a little while—Mom generally gave us about thirty seconds. Then she'd chirp, "Let's play the Glad Game!" and we'd have to list all the things that were still great about our lives. This became a lifelong habit for me. I just can't stay focused on the negative for very long.

Pulling yourself out of a quagmire of problems requires positive action. And you only take positive action when you focus your thinking on positive future outcomes rather than present challenges and failures. It takes practice, just like a musician practices scales, but you can train yourself to do it.

Here's a note I received from a friend of mine who shared how she played the Glad Game one afternoon:

I was driving on the freeway when my tire blew out. I was very nervous and tried to remember everything to do. You read with time and leisure in the Automobile Club Journal what to do when your car spins out or your tire blows out on you. Of course, when it happens, you are just reacting. Well, once I pulled over, I began to play the Glad Game that I learned from you—thank you!

I was glad because: 1) it was one o'clock in the afternoon, 2) it was in a well traveled area, 3) I had my cell phone with me and could get a signal (what a concept), 4) I was already in the right lane and could pull safely over to the roadside, 5) I was only going thirty miles an hour, 6) I was at the exit right near my house, 7) a road angel came by from Cal Trans who "happened" to be five minutes behind me and assisted me, 8) the service was free and they do not accept tips or anything, 9) I was not hit by any passing motorists, 10) I got my car repaired that day and they gave me a rental car so I could finish my work for the day, 11) it occurred on a day that I do not see patients so I lost no time from actual patient visits and therefore income, 12) I still had time to go to my WRS meeting where I saw you! That's twelve reasons to be glad.

Thank you always and love, Lynn Kerew, D.C.

Life has good things and bad things, all mixed together, a grab bag of highs and lows. In *Illusions,* Richard Bach wrote that everything in life was either fun or learning. So if something happens that isn't fun, look for the lesson. And if you'd rather have more fun, focus your mind on what's good in your life. You can be happy or you can be depressed. Here's the prescription for both:

Recipe for depression:
1) Think about yourself.
2) Think about what you don't have.
3) Think about what you're afraid will happen.
Recipe for happiness:
1) Think about helping others.
2) Think about everything good that you have.
3) Think about your next "I can hardly wait!"

Everything That Happens Isn't About You

We always think everything that happens is about us. Because we're the star of our movie, right? But we are also co-stars and supporting players in other people's movies. Sometimes the things that happen are for someone else's benefit, and we are put in their path in order to help them.

It was a bright summer day, and I was zipping down Kenter Street, off to an appointment. Everyone zips down Kenter—it's a wide residential street, and in the many years I've been living in this area, never have I seen a policeman. Until now. Uh oh. Well, I admit it, I was zipping along a bit too fast, and the slow car in front of me just wasn't pulling over fast enough, so I zipped around him over the double yellow lines…oops.

Seeing the flashing lights on the police car behind me right away, I turned into a side street and parked. I got my driver's license, registration, and insurance card ready, because I knew the drill. Experienced, you see?

The police officer walked up to my window, smiled at me, and asked if I knew how fast I was going.

"Um, fast?" I smiled back sheepishly.

"You were going fifty," he said. "Do you know what the speed limit is?"

"Uh…slow?" The officer wasn't amused.

He said, "Thirty." We both knew I was toast.

He next explained that I also zipped over the double yellow lines, which is a very big no-no. Oh dear. Burnt toast.

The officer said he was going to write me a ticket and asked for my documents. I said, "I understand," and gave him what he needed. As he walked away to write it up, I shrugged mentally and decided I wasn't going to let this glitch in my day ruin my day. I played the Glad Game. I know I drive fast, more often than I should, and have to pay the piper for that occasionally, so why be angry or upset about it? The officer is just doing his job, and he's being nice and friendly doing it, so okay. And it's a beautiful day, I have plenty of time to get where I'm going, I'm going to have a great lunch with a good friend, and so on.

He walked back, ticket in hand, and told me that he was going to give me a break on the speeding and only wrote me a ticket for the double yellow line infraction. I knew that saved me a bundle, so I thanked him very much. Then, in a flash of intuition, or just because I instinctively wanted to return good for good, I offered him a copy of *The Wealthy Spirit* that was sitting on the seat beside me. (It was after I had received the ticket, so it couldn't be considered a bribe, just a thank you.) He was very sweet and thanked me and asked me to sign it for him, which I was happy to do. We shook hands, smiled, and wished each other a pleasant day.

As I turned my car around and started to drive past him, he called out for me to stop for a moment. I pulled my car up to his and rolled down my window. "What is it?" I asked.

With a wondering look on his face, he held up my book and said, "I've been looking for a book like this for four months. I even went to the bookstore yesterday, looking for a book on finance, but didn't see anything I wanted and left empty-handed. This is exactly the book I've been searching for to help me work on my finances. Thank you so much!"

Lemon Meringue. I've never felt quite so good after getting a ticket.

There are other people on the planet. Everything that happens isn't about you. Sometimes you've just been thrown on the deck in order to save another sailor from drowning. This incident was clearly both: he needed my book, and I needed his reminder to drive more safely. If we look for the mutual benefits we provide each other in every transaction, we can find them. The master design of life works beautifully.

> **There are other people on the planet. Everything that happens isn't about you.**

Years ago, when Mikhail Baryshnikov was at the height of his dancing prowess, he made an appearance with the American Ballet Theater at the Dorothy Chandler Pavilion in Los Angeles. My boyfriend Stan and I got tickets to a matinee performance of *Giselle* months in advance and looked forward to the show with eager "I can hardly waits."

On performance day, we dressed our best, and plunked ourselves happily in our orchestra seats. "This is so great!" I beamed happily, and Stan nodded.

Then the announcer's voice rang through the auditorium. "I regret to inform you that Mr. Baryshnikov was injured at a rehearsal this morning and will be unable to perform in this afternoon's ballet.

You aren't always in charge of what happens, but you are always in charge of your response to what happens.

The part will be performed by…" the rest of what he said was overwhelmed by the chorus of boos and "Oh nos!" from the audience.

I sighed unhappily and turned to Stan. "So how did we create this happening?" I asked. We were both learning about taking personal responsibility for everything in our lives, and I was overdoing it a bit.

"Oh, Chellie," scoffed Stan, "we didn't create this. We're just here to balance the energy and help everyone else get past it."

I loved that. It was a perfect illustration of the concept that you aren't always in charge of what happens, but you are always in charge of your response to what happens. So we lightened up, meditated, and sent loving, healing energy to Misha, his understudy, the other dancers, and the disappointed audience.

I don't know if it helped anyone else, but it sure helped us.

So look around at the other people involved whenever you suffer a disappointment. What can you do to ameliorate the situation? Can you get beyond yourself and reach out to help others? When you do, you'll find you help yourself more than anyone else.

Swimming Lessons

When the ships are sinking, we have to learn how to swim. Here is an excerpt from a newsletter I sent out to my e-zine subscribers in the fall of 2004:

Ship ahoy!

Isn't it fun to see ships coming in after you've worked hard to build them and send them out? Sometimes you think they must have gotten lost at sea, hit an iceberg, or sunk. Then surprise! A couple of ships come sailing into port after all. But you notice they're not exactly the same ships you sent out…

A few weeks ago, in quick succession, several ships came into my harbor. An email arrived from Susan Medwied, who said she had been asked to write about "Essential Books for the Woman Entrepreneur" for Entrepreneur *magazine, and* The Wealthy Spirit *was one of her selections. Then I received a call from* Starting Over, *the popular day-time reality TV show, to be a guest financial expert on the show. The day after I taped that show, I was contacted "out of the blue" and booked on the radio show* Marketplace *on NPR.*

These weren't ships that I had directly sent out—I hadn't called the magazine, the TV show, or NPR to pitch them. But I had pitched other shows and other magazines and been turned down. I thought the ships were sunk. But no ships are totally lost—positive energy out always results in positive energy in, somehow, sometime, someplace. It's the law of cause and effect and 'what goes around comes around'… The Entrepreneur *ship came in because Susan was reading my book when the opportunity to suggest books for the article came to her. The* Starting Over *ship came in because one of the stars of the show, Rhonda Britten, has been a friend of mine for years and suggested me to the producers. The NPR ship came in because "a colleague recommended your book." Writing the book was the big cruise ship that took years to build. Speaking and networking and doing PR every month for the past two years were the hundreds of little tugboats sent out to help the big cruise ship make it into port.*

Keep the faith! Your ships are still out there, even if you can't see them. They are still headed for your dock.

One Ship Sunk, One Lost at Sea

Right after I sent out that announcement, every ship I had bragged about coming in—sank. At first I was terribly embarrassed. Here I had told the world all this great stuff was happening for me, and all of it had just landed in the drink. How humiliating!

But then I started to laugh. And then I started writing the next newsletter:

"Ship ahoy!" comes the cry from the crow's nest! Followed by "Oops…"

Do you find your email inbox flooded with proud announcements of awards, good PR, new contracts, new classes starting, newsy newsletters full of "My ship has come in!" stories? Me, too. I like happy stories and mine are usually pretty gleeful and filled with exclamation points—so that one reader snidely pointed out, "You look like you just got asked to the prom and you couldn't wait to email your friends." Yeah, that's right! I like that feeling and emailing all my buddies…

This one is different. It's a sunken ship announcement.

A few weeks ago, in quick succession, several ships appeared on the horizon. Entrepreneur *magazine was going to write a review of my book, the TV show* Starting Over *was going to have me as a guest financial expert on the show, and I was booked on the radio show*

Marketplace *on NPR. Wow, I was excited! I wrote up an announcement for all of you and proudly trumpeted my news.*

Promptly after that, one of my new ships sank. My television appearance ended up on the cutting room floor. Shoot. It's never fun when ships sink, but it's particularly annoying when they sink at the dock while you're unloading it. Then the radio show I taped turned out to be a local show in Florida, not Marketplace, *which has an audience of millions. And it aired during the middle of a hurricane. Okay, so it's a leaky canoe instead of a cruise ship, but maybe somebody heard it and bought a book...As for the* Entrepreneur *magazine article, we have called the Coast Guard, and they are out scouring the seas on a search and rescue mission...*

Oh, well, in the entertainment industry they have an expression for it—"That's showbiz!" And as Jack Canfield told me, here's the four-letter word to use when ships sink: "Next!" Because the Universe now owes me a ship, don't you think?

Don't give up the ships! Keep sending them out, even in the face of icebergs and disasters. Babe Ruth hit more home runs than any other baseball player of his era—and he also struck out more times than any other player. The price of success is failure. Successful people are just willing to fail more often than most people. Did you know that the average millionaire has filed bankruptcy 3.5 times? Walt Disney filed twice. William Macy, founder of Macy's department stores, filed seven times before he was successful. Mark Victor Hansen has a bankruptcy in his past, and so do I. If we can recover from it, move on, and become successful, so can you.

So take heart when some of your ships sink. Because there are others that may not be at the dock just yet, but they are just over the horizon, laden with treasure, and sailing home to you. No energy is lost;

every positive step taken is rewarded. The ship that comes in may look different than the ship you sent out, but you earned every bit of treasure in its hold.

Dolphins Will Save You from Drowning

An amazing thing happened then. In the next twenty-four hours, I was completely overwhelmed with responses to that newsletter. Whereas I usually received twenty-five to thirty congratulatory messages when I send out notices about good news, my "Sinking Ships" letter got over 160 replies. Here is a sampling of some of the delightful responses I received from the Dolphins in my pod, filled with clever ship analogies.

Ahoy matey! Fear not, there be yachts and dinghies at your pier! Thanks for sharing this. Lise

I'm so sorry to hear about the sunken ship. It's more than disappointing when you think it's going to happen and then it doesn't. A year ago, LHJ magazine was supposed to do a story on us. I was pumped, and then a couple of months later, I was deflated. The ship sank. Bummer, big time... I just wanted you to know that I have an extra life jacket if you need it, and I'm always willing to share my own personal life raft with you—anytime. Your friend, Suzanne

Thank you for making me feel not so alone and for helping me laugh about sunk ships. I've had interviews in the past three months with Nightline and CNN and both got cut, so while I want to scream out loud, I have tossed them up to a good experience and said, 'Next!' Thanks again for the stress reliever. Liz

Thank you for this. I've had a couple of ships sink recently (I got cut out of the final edit of a People magazine article, for one).

I really needed this…I'll just keep sending them out. A fan, Donna

I think what was so powerful about your email was that those of us who have taken your class look at you as someone who is immune to having a ship sink. You reminded us all that even your harbor sometimes has a dry dock, and as disappointing as that might be, you feel it, acknowledge it, and then keep going. Rebecca

Great email. Good reminders, and we were able to see your human disappointment and your vulnerability and honesty, but along with that your hopeful spirit. Even if some ships didn't come back—that doesn't mean that the ship captains out there are not talking about you! From their conversation some new opportunities might come! Love, Gail

Keep swimming! Thanks for sharing your "sunken ship" stories. Yes, I for one, think the universe will send you some floatable ships. We've all had similar experiences and could feel your splashes of wet water. Judy

You are my role model, not because of your many and ongoing successes, but because of how you handle your sunken ships. I have had a similar week and your email arrived at the perfect time! Both cruise ships are circling the harbor! Love, Victoria

The Queen Mary is sailing your way, Chellie! Get your wide-brimmed hat ready! Gratefully yours, Cathy

How can you continue to feel bad about a few silly sunken ships when you are surrounded by loving friends like these? It was a great lesson to me to continue to open up, to be vulnerable, that sometimes love comes more easily to you when you need a shoulder to cry on and a cup of tea than when the world is cheering you from the stands. We think we get love from being fabulous and successful and rich, but that isn't it. Sometimes that's an impenetrable wall that keeps people isolated. Being perfect is not the best way to reach people. Being vulnerable is. People want to know you need them. People want to know you're like them. Everyone has sinking ships, everyone cries in the night, everyone needs a pat on the back and a hanky upon occasion. Your Dolphin friends love to be there for you when they can see through the chinks in your walls to your tender heart within. Open up. Let them in.

We think we get love from being fabulous and successful and rich, but that isn't it. Being perfect is not the best way to reach people.

Most of these examples are small, personal ones from my own experience. But they work the same in larger contexts, too. Look at the world's reaction to the tsunami that killed over 200,000 people in December 2004 and destroyed so many families, homes, and businesses in Sri Lanka, Indonesia, and other Southeast Asian countries. In their suffering, they were all Our People, and countries all over the world jumped in to help, sent money, sent teams of doctors, sent love and prayers. Nine months later, when New Orleans was stricken by Hurricane Katrina, 90 percent of the city was flooded. Sri Lanka, a small nation still in recovery from its own disaster, sent $25,000 to help America, the world super power. I cried when I read that, it touched me so deeply.

Human beings are so resilient! We suffer, but we recover. Ten days after Katrina, flood waters still high, New Orleans business leaders banded together to discuss reopening their famed French Quarter and started planning their next Mardi Gras celebration. *Laissez les bon temps roulez!* I've got my Mardi Gras beads ready.

The Truth Will Set You Free—But First, It Will Scare You Silly

In the beginning of teaching my workshops, I focused on just the good things I knew and could exemplify. I stayed away from the sticky wickets—the fact that I had been in abusive relationships, the fact that I had filed bankruptcy and lost a home to foreclosure, the fact that I had abused alcohol to the point that I had to get myself to Alcoholics Anonymous to get sober.

But a funny thing happened when I started to share these things. A couple in my class was struggling with their debts and considering bankruptcy. I was trying to help them determine what to do, when the young man looked at me petulantly and said, "Well, easy for you to say, but you've never been in these circumstances, have you?"

It was the first time I had been directly confronted with the issue in class, and suddenly I knew I couldn't hide it anymore. I said, "Yes, I have, and I filed bankruptcy."

I looked around at a group of shocked faces and then poured out my story. I had always told the beginning of the story, like I did at the beginning of this chapter: how my biggest client in my business management firm had left with only two weeks notice and how I scrambled to save my business and started teaching financial workshops.

What I hadn't shared was how I borrowed $50,000 on credit cards to save the company, how I had tried to pay it back over the next five years, and how the 19.8 percent interest ate me

> **Human beings are so resilient! We suffer, but we recover.**

alive. I hadn't told them I lived on Low Budget for years, and when my budget failed or a client didn't pay me, I borrowed even more on the credit cards, because by then it was a habit to borrow. I hadn't

told how I drank to cope, and drank more to sleep. Or how humili-
ated I felt to be the president of a leading women's organization,
owner of a bookkeeping service, and teaching Financial Stress
Reduction workshops—and I was the most financially stressed person in the room. Or how filing bankruptcy and going to Alcoholics
Anonymous got me sober in money and sober in drink and got me
started on the road to financial, physical, and mental recovery.

From hope and faith, action is born. And when you have faith and take action, you can produce miracles.

But this day I told it all. I told
them how I faced my own
demons and recognized that
every principle I was teaching in
my workshops was something I
wasn't doing in my own life. My
students had all been improv-
ing—they were making more money, having more fun, and doing
more good. But I wasn't. What was the difference between them and
me? They were following the instructions and doing what I told
them to do. They were doing affirmations every day—I wasn't even
doing that. I saw as I talked to them what had to change: *I* had to
change.

That day, I humbly enrolled myself in my own course. I took
every class with them. I listened to every instruction I gave—and then
followed it. And my life improved dramatically. My income doubled
in six months. I was happier, richer, more fulfilled, and more at peace
with myself.

But the biggest change was in my students. They heard my story
and knew I had suffered just like they had, that I had made mistakes
just like theirs, that I wasn't perfect, that I wasn't born with a silver
tongue or a silver spoon in my mouth. I was just like them. And if I

could use these tools to turn my life around, then they could, too. It gave them more hope, and it gave them more faith. From hope and faith, action is born. And when you have faith and take action, you can produce miracles. Or you just put yourself in the way of miracles. It seemed to me that everyone who took my class after I began telling the truth had bigger successes. I certainly did.

I'm not saying you should wash all your dirty linen on your résumé or dry it in the boardroom. I am a teacher and the best illustration I know is how the principles I teach worked for me first, and then how they worked for others. When you see that, you see how they can work for you. Look within your own life and see where honesty and vulnerability might reach Your People in ways that being high on a pedestal won't. Tell of the things you know and how you know it. Admit the things you don't know and ask others if they do.

We are all drowning sometimes. But our lifesavers are all around us. Reach out for them. Sharing the truth with others strengthens you in ways both seen and unseen. Lifting each other up, we survive another day—until one day we reach the shore.

Strategy 8 | Lighten Up on the Way to Enlightenment

"The universe is full of magical things patiently waiting for our wits to grow sharper."
—Eden Phillpotts

Part of being a Zillionaire is knowing that life isn't just about you, your money, your happiness, and your life. It isn't just about your family, your friends, and your city, either. Thomas Friedman's book *The World is Flat* proclaims that fiber optics and the digital revolution have connected us all: China can send material to Brazil where a Dutch company has a plant that uses American subcontractors and data processors in India, and vice versa, ad infinitum. With all of our different backgrounds, traditions, beliefs, creeds, and colors, we have to learn to work and live together. In order to do this, we need an overhaul of some of our traditional thinking and behavior. There are 6.3 billion people on our green Earth, and each one deserves a chance to grow and prosper. A Zillionaire can see a person's inner Dolphin, regardless of the language they speak or the clothing they wear.

A Zillionaire Life

"It's a great day for science!" said Bob Hayes as he bustled his students into the classroom at Millikan Middle School. For thirty-nine years, that was his standard morning greeting.

Folks who knew him said his was always the cheeriest voice in the room. Whenever a new teacher or substitute started work, he was the one greeting them at the door of the teachers lounge. Whenever someone needed help, he was the first in line to offer assistance. He treated everyone as though he was the host of the party and they were honored guests.

Bob lived down the street from my sister, Carole, and bonded with her nine-year-old son, Nick. Bob never passed up the opportunity to teach Nick something: about the lizard Nick was holding, their German shepherd, or whatever came to his teacher's mind when he jogged by. But one day he was jogging and collapsed. He never got up again.

There are 6.3 billion people on our green Earth, and each one deserves a chance to grow and prosper.

The school hallways were silent; no more "it's a great day for science" shouts rang there. As the word of his passing spread, the condolences poured in to the family. "Mr. Hayes died?" one woman asked. "Oh no. He's the reason I became a nurse." The day of his memorial service, nearly five hundred people came to pay their last respects. People stood one by one and told how Mr. Hayes had shaped their lives: "He's the reason I became a teacher." "He's the reason I stayed in school." "He's the reason I got into college." "He's the reason..." "He's the reason..." For three hours, people shared their stories of this beautiful man, of his kindness and goodwill.

One story stood out from the rest. His son Bobby told how he noticed his dad took his change out of his pocket every night and put it on his dresser. One day, he saw that among the pennies and the quarters lay a solitary gold coin. It had a Boy Scout emblem engraved on one side, and on the other it said something like, "Put me in your left pocket in the morning, then move me to your right pocket when you've done your good deed for the day." From the testimony given at the memorial service, it seems clear he didn't stop at just one. Good deeds became his habit. Good deeds became who he was.

> **It isn't necessary to try to change the world—just look forty houses to your left and forty houses to your right, and try to help those people.**

I've heard that in Buddhism, it isn't necessary to try to change the world—just look forty houses to your left and forty houses to your right, and try to help those people. If everyone did just that, the world would be a peaceful place. If everyone started the day with "It's a great day for science" or "It's a great day for bookkeeping" or teaching or ballet or music or learning or whatever you have to do, the world would be so much brighter.

The world is a little dimmer now that Bob Hayes has left it. But his mourners left the memorial service uplifted and inspired instead of despondent. They had borne witness to a life well-lived and been moved. Perhaps some of them will get a little gold coin, put it in their left pocket each morning, and move it to their right somewhere before the end of each day.

Your People—Your God

My friend Adipen Bose said to me, "People say that in India we have eight million gods. That's not it—we have eight million *aspects* of God." That sounds right to me. If there is a God, Creative Consciousness, Higher Power, Divine Designer of the Universe—call it "The Force" as in *Star Wars*—when we small humans touch upon such magnificence, can we be entrusted to see all of the mighty power contained therein? Most likely not. So what we do is choose aspects of God to worship, pray to, or be mindful of, and we choose groups called religions in order to bond with others and touch the Divine: Jewish, Hindu, Catholic, Protestant, Mormon, Muslim, Church of Religious Science, Ba H'ai, et al. (There was a survey in England in which 390,000 people listed their religious affiliation as "Jedi." The aspect of God I believe in would be laughing heartily with me about that!)

I am an equal opportunity believer.

I think it grand that so many people gather together in ancient traditions to celebrate the higher good in humanity and nature. Find Your Group of Your People, bond with them, and connect with spirit often. The part we need to leave behind is when we condemn Other People for joining other groups that follow different traditions. A survey conducted by Harris Interactive in 2004 showed that 69 percent of adult Americans believe religious differences are the biggest hurdle to global peace. Since it doesn't appear that all 6.3 billion of us are going to agree on One True Religion anytime soon, we must somehow learn how to agree to disagree, smile, and wave to each other across the altars of our choosing.

The Bible, the Koran, the Upanishads, the Vedanta, the Sufi stories, the Torah, the Course in Miracles, Science of Mind, the readings of Edgar Cayce at the Association for Research and Enlightenment, and all other spiritual writings are tales of someone's experience of the Divine. Each offers a perspective and help in finding Your People and Your Aspect of God. Follow the path that sings to you, join the group that feels like home to you—and let everyone else do the same. Let all of us who believe in a Higher Power happily bond with all the others who believe in one, too, whatever hymn they choose to sing.

I am an equal opportunity believer. I believe in Jesus, Buddha, Mohammed, Yahweh, Gandhi, Krishna, Lakshmi, the Dali Lama, Mary Magdalene, Mother Teresa, Paramahansa Yogananda, Ernest Holmes, the Pope, Martin Luther, Martin Luther King Jr., elves, fairies, Frodo, Han Solo, Intelligent Design, and Darwin. I believe in Bob Hayes. I believe in my mom and dad and my sisters. I believe in you, I believe in me. I believe in the Universal Good in all religious traditions. Their instructions about how to be a good person are very similar: love God, love your fellow man, give to the poor, help the downtrodden, don't lie, don't cheat, don't steal, don't kill, and treat others as you would like them to treat you. It seems to me how we get there is not quite as important as getting there. As Deng Ming-Dao says in *365 Tao*, "When you buy something that has assembly instructions, you follow the directions, but you do not then venerate the instructions."

> "When you buy something that has assembly instructions, you follow the directions, but you do not then venerate the instructions."

A Zillion Roads to Take Us Home

There is beauty to be found and appreciated in all religious traditions. I gained insight from Sufi stories, I learned compassion and love from Jesus, I learned basic morality from the Ten Commandments of the Torah. Catholics have beautiful cathedrals, a wonderful liturgy, Gregorian Chants, and the Sistine Chapel. The Mormons I have met have been some of the nicest people I've ever encountered. Muslims pray five times a day, and the muezzin's song calling the faithful to worship is profoundly beautiful. I found Tao in the night-blooming jasmine outside my door and the purring of the cat in my arms. I embraced reincarnation after reading about Edgar Cayce's work in *There is a River* by Thomas Sugrue, because it rang an internal bell for me. Many lives, many chances to discover and learn the truth—I like that idea.

I listen to everyone and do the best I can to make my own decisions, to take the wheat and leave the chaff behind. Someone huffed at me that I couldn't just believe the parts of religions I liked and disregard the rest. Sure I can. Just watch me keep the baby Dolphin and throw the Sharky bits in the bathwater out. Aren't you going to do the same thing with this book—use the parts of it that work for you and disregard the rest? Some people sneer at "cafeteria-style spirituality," but I like it. You can put the forty-nine-bean soup instead of plain lentil on my tray every day, and if I want to pick out the lima beans, I get to.

Use the parts of this book that work for you and disregard the rest.

I've always been just a wee bit suspicious when told that God doesn't want me to think for myself but just play "Follow the Leader."

One afternoon, I was at an airport, ready to catch my plane back home. It was crowded—lots of lines, lots of security check points. My friend Shelley and I automatically joined a very long line, three people deep, waiting to go up an escalator nearly fifty yards away. I looked ahead and noticed something unusual. Escalators are usually built in pairs, with one going up and one going down. There were two escalators here, but both of them were going up. Yet no one in this long, long line had noticed that there were *two up* escalators. Everyone was crowding in line waiting for the one on the right-hand side. I looked around for a sign that said the other one was broken, to see if it wasn't moving, or if there was some obvious reason why no one was using it. There was nothing.

I tapped the young man in front of me on the shoulder and asked, "Do you see any reason why no one is using the other up escalator?"

His eyes widened, and he looked sharply at the escalators. He turned back to me laughingly, shook his head, and said, "No, I don't," straightened his shoulders and motioned to me, "Let's go!"

Shelley and I followed and we walked past sixty-plus people waiting in line for the right escalator, got on the left escalator, and zipped right to the top.

I think religions are like that. It's comfortable to follow in the line in front of you. It's a habit and it feels safe. Usually, there's some charismatic salesman up ahead, pointing the way, saying, "This one is the right escalator." He's got a group following him already, and it seems natural to join the crowd. This can be fun; everyone can chat with each other and party. Just beware when they start saying, "This is the *only* escalator." That's the sales and marketing team creating a sense of urgency for their membership drive. That's about power and money (theirs), not about God and Spirit.

Take another look: There are a zillion people on a zillion escalators, all going up.

To Believe or Not to Believe, That Is the Question

If there's no scientific proof, why believe in any God, religion, or spiritual tradition at all?

A man from Chicago emailed me one afternoon: *I enjoyed your book, some good stuff. One thing that disturbed me slightly: your constant reference to God. I don't think God blesses people with money, if there even is a God. That's my next point. If you ask people to turn to God for things, you might also ask them to turn to Martians or the "tunnel people." Not everyone believes in God. Religion belongs in churches, not self-help books. Why is it if you believe in Martians, you're a wacko? If you believe in a guy in the sky, you're "on the right path."*

St. Augustine said that if you only had one prayer each day and that was "Thank you!" it would be enough.

It's not a matter of praying to God for things, but sending thanks heavenward for all blessings already received. I appreciate whatever Higher Power gave me the blessing of life and all the good that flows from that. If you don't believe in God, thank fate, thank your mom and dad, or thank your lucky stars. St. Augustine said that if you only had one prayer each day and that was "Thank you!" it would be enough. Studies have shown that, so far, the only thing they can prove makes people happier is spending time each day writing down all the things for which they are grateful. Focusing on what you have, instead of what you don't have, makes you more energetic, more enthusiastic, more alert, and healthier. More Dolphin. My bet is, richer, too. More Zillionaire.

I didn't ask him who the "tunnel people" were…

Living as a Zillionaire means choosing beliefs that make you happy. Whether or not there actually is a God is shrouded in mystery. If you don't think there's any proof of God, you won't find any. If you think there is proof, you'll find some. And since there are many Gods available to choose from, might I suggest you choose a Dolphin kind of loving God instead of a Sharky, angry, warlike God? Or maybe it's time for a Goddess? I was brought up with the Father, the Son, and the Holy Ghost, but wouldn't it be nice to include the Mother, the Daughter, and Women's Intuition? The female principle needs a little more good press. We're tired of just being the villain of the Garden of Eden story. At least Eve was brave enough to consider the options and take a risk. Adam just whined, "The woman made me do it." Sheesh, Adam, you're such a Tuna.

Thou Shalt Lighten Up!

"All the problems of the world result from too much Seriousness," John Morton wrote. "Scientists from the Clown Academy have already discovered a new source of healing…the Clown Chakra. If people are feeling miserable, if they have financial problems, if their relationship situation is the pits, if they are in ill health, if they have a need to sue people, if they find fault with their brother, then obviously, their Clown Chakra is closed. When this happens…the cells of every organ display a sad face, and when the Clown Chakra is open and functioning normally, the cells display a happy face."

I smile every time I read that passage. If you have trouble being open-minded, you can at least be open-Clown-Chakraed. Thank God for clowns, comedians, and jokesters who keep us from dying of terminal Seriousness. Let's send love and smiling faces to everyone around us—including ourselves—and we'll help everyone keep their Clown Chakras functioning happily.

Here's a story to help you laugh: three people died and found themselves in Hell, with burning agony all around them. Horrified, the first man wailed, "I knew I should have been a better person!"

The second man broke down and cried, "I knew I should have gone to church every Sunday!"

The New Ager just sat down in Lotus Position and said, "It's not hot, and I'm not here."

Believe what you want and laugh. A friend of mine who is Roman Catholic was concerned when she fell in love with a Jewish man, and spoke to her priest about it. He laid her anxieties to rest when he told her, "Same book, different chapter."

I loved that. Give me openness, give me freedom, give me tolerance.

The Wealth of Nations Is in Our Diversity

On vacation in Memphis, Tennessee, I visited the Civil Rights Museum, set in the Lorraine Motel where Martin Luther King Jr. was assassinated. I sat in a bus similar to the one Rosa Parks sat in and listened to the harsh orders over the loudspeaker that she had been given to relinquish her seat to a white man. A wreath adorned the balcony railing where Martin fell, shot dead; his room was preserved just as it had been that day. Across the street, you could look out the window where James Earl Ray had stood to make his fateful shot. A wall in that room was dedicated to other great leaders around the world who fought and died in the service of humanity. Many are the martyrs, with different names, in different colors, from different cultures. All with one message—let us embrace each other and live in peace.

When we packed our bags, headed for the airport and home once more, we listened with sad irony as the young black man who drove our van complained about the town's influx of Middle Eastern taxi drivers, how they were bad for business, how they had strange names, how their writing looked like chicken scratches. And we saw how prejudice never fades—it just changes colors. It comes from fear of the Other, fear that they will take over, fear there won't be enough for everyone, fear that they will change the status quo. Fear comes from ignorance, from Zero thinking, and from negative affirmations passed down for generations. The Golden Rule becomes the Iron Rule: Do unto others before they do it unto you. Angry Tuna follow Angry Sharks and the result is war.

> **Prejudice comes from fear of the Other, fear that they will take over, fear there won't be enough for everyone, fear that they will change the status quo. Fear comes from ignorance, from Zero thinking.**

We've been fighting and killing each other forever on this planet over bits of land and tendrils of ideology. Murder, thievery, intolerance, hatred, and genocide re-root on a regular cycle, like some dark bulb that snakes out a poison stem with every spring thaw. There's genocide in the Bible, when Joshua was exhorted to kill every man, woman, and child in Jericho. Hitler and his minions killed six million people just sixty years ago. The Rwandan genocide killed one million a scarce decade ago, and Darfur was just last week. What will be next week?

Dolphins can fight, and do. But when we have to go to war to contain the Angry Sharks, we have already lost. War only sows more hatred among the vanquished, and they chant their negative affirmations for eons. How long have the Catholics and the Protestants in Northern Ireland been fighting? The Serbs and the Bosnians? The Arabs and the Jews? The Armenians and the Turks? The Montagues and the Capulets? The Hatfields and the McCoys?

We should take the suggestion of the *Guerrilla Girls*: "The world needs a new weapon: the estrogen bomb. Imagine: you drop it on the area of violent conflict, and men throw down their guns, hug each other, apologize, say it was all their fault, and then start to clean up the mess."

Zillionaires care nothing for country or origin, or language, or dress, or religion. They don't care if you're black, white, red, yellow, green, or polka dot. Zillionaires only care that you're a Dolphin.

> **Zillionaires care nothing for country or origin, or language, or dress, or religion.**

The answer to world peace and prosperity is more Dolphin-in-training programs. Most people are Tuna. There are Dolphin Leaders and Shark Leaders, but there are no Tuna Leaders. When we all learn Dolphin behavior and gain confidence in ourselves and our place in the world, we overcome fear and replace it with appreciation. Globalization is here; billions are connected through the Internet, cell phones, and cable. High tide floats all boats, but we have to make sure everyone's vessels are seaworthy. Zillionaires everywhere need to not just give fish, but teach fishing.

Teach Dolphins-in-training to read books, take classes, visit museums, explore other cultures, and learn from other Dolphin pods. Take them to watch foreign films—subtitled only, so that they can hear the cadences and emotion in another tongue. Encourage them to travel, take vacations, see more of life. Give them perspective. Teach them the errors of the prejudices of the past that they might join with you to help create a better future where all are welcome. Let them see that not all life is lived as they live it, and to celebrate the diversity that makes life fascinating and rich. Dolphins come in many styles and colors. A *THX 1138* world in which everyone is bald and wears white is not a fun world.

Someone told me once that "no one goes to Heaven until everybody goes." That statement instantly enlarged my picture of the world, and I felt a personal responsibility to everyone in it. I wanted to help others find enlightenment and answers to Universal Truths. Oh dear. In my arrogance, I thought I knew the way and tried to point it out to others in order to help them see it.

Then, one morning, a humbling thought struck me. Maybe I wasn't supposed to be helping everyone else "get it." Maybe *I* was supposed to get it. Maybe all of you are ready to go to heaven already, and I'm the last one on the planet who hasn't gotten it yet. Oops. My pride came crashing down in *that* fall. So now I share with you my work along this path, with the hope that I am getting it. If you don't think I am, maybe there is hope in the future, because I am working on it, along with you.

The Zillionaire View of the Universe

If you sit in your home and look only at your family, you will have a limited view of the Universe. If you stand in your yard and expand your vision to your neighborhood, the view shifts. Enlarge your vision to your city, your state, your nation, and it shifts again.

Now look up to the stars and tell me your place in the Universe.

One of the obstacles preventing us from having balance and perspective in our lives today is that we don't connect to the larger

Universe each night, as our ancient counterparts did. The bright lights of the city drown the starlight and we don't get a nightly reminder of the limitlessness of space and time. Or humanity's place in it.

In my workshop, I hold up a photo taken in outer space by the Hubble Space Telescope of our galaxy, the Milky Way.

"How many stars are in a galaxy?" I ask.

"Millions," some participants respond. "Billions?" ask others. Some just look at me blankly. They don't think about the stars.

"Billions and billions," I reply, in my best Carl Sagan imitation. "There are approximately one hundred billion stars in one galaxy."

The number doesn't quite register with the group. It's too big.

> **There are billions of human beings on this planet Earth. Surely we have vested interest in helping each other. But there isn't enough sharing going on.**

Then I turn the page, and show them the picture of the Hubble Field, with its several hundred *galaxies* never before seen. Jaws drop a little at that. I tell them how amazed I was at this picture when I first saw it. How I took it to a family gathering and showed my dad, who worked in the space program all his life. "Yes," he smiled, "but that's just a small corner of the sky in that picture. If you take a sewing needle, hold it at arm's length and look through its eye, that's the area that's covered in this picture. Now multiply."

A hush falls in my classroom then, and together we ponder the enormity of it all, the vastness of space and the smallness of us.

And we're all alone here…?

Perhaps. But if we're all alone, it's a very big miracle. And if we're not alone, that's a big miracle, too.

We don't know for sure, yet. But we do know that there are billions of human beings on this planet Earth. Surely we have a vested interest in helping each other. But there isn't enough sharing going on. A *Time* magazine cover feature on poverty stated that three billion of our fellow human beings live in poverty, 1.1 billion people live in extreme poverty, and eight million people die each year because they are too poor to survive.

And you're complaining about—what?

After scrambling for your three square meals a day and a roof over your head, you're in the habit of scrambling, so next you scramble for gourmet dinners and a fancier roof. We love to use our creative juices to get more and better stuff—it's how we road test our powers of creation. That's all fine and wonderful. But what is your life's purpose? What gives it meaning beyond accumulation of *stuff*?

> **Three billion of our fellow human beings live in poverty, 1.1 billion people live in extreme poverty, and eight million people die each year because they are too poor to survive. And you're complaining about—what?**

At your funeral service, do you want them to be saying, "She had the best clothes" or "He had the most money"? Or do you want them to say, "He brought joy to so many" or "She helped a lot of people"? Do you think they will miss your big house and fancy car? Do you think they will care what title you had on your business card? Or will they miss your smile, your comfort, your love, your Sunday dinners? Did you have a gold coin in your pocket?

Troy Driscoll, 15, and his friend Josh Long, 17, were lost at sea in a tiny boat when it was caught in a riptide that carried them far out in the ocean. After three days, the search and rescue team gave up, thinking they were both dead. But miraculously, after six and a half days, they were accidentally found by a fishing boat one hundred miles from where they started.

During their agonizing journey, they had clung to each other for warmth, prayed, and sang hymns. When one's courage would fail and speak of death, the other would say no, hang on.

When they were rescued, Troy said, "We talked about reality, how it hits you in the face. In normal life, you're always thinking about getting a better life. But when you're out there, and you have nothing but water, you think that [everyday existence] is a millionaire's life."

That's a Zillionaire perspective.

Tithing Is Sharing

Zillionaires know they have a zillionaire's life and they share their wealth. Tithing is giving a portion of your money, goods, and riches to God. The traditional recommended portion for tithing is 10 percent—not 50 percent or 90 percent—just 10 percent. Balance is important. It's not about giving everything away, but sharing a portion of the good you have acquired. I know people who overdo tithing to the point where they can't pay their own bills. That's Tuna behavior. But the fact is, if you belong to a religious group, they are going to need contributions from their membership in order to pay their worldly bills and do good works. So ante up. Be a contributor. A church in Las Vegas often gets gaming chips in the collection plate on Sundays. They assign a junior monk to go the various casinos and redeem the chips for cash. They call him the Chip Monk. Clown Chakra open!

Give chips, give cash, give service, give time. Call it tithing or call it sharing. Be of service somewhere in your spiritual life where you do it for the love of your fellow beings without regard to monetary compensation. It only makes sense to share. It's great when you're rich and happy, but isn't life a lot more fun when you have lots of friends who are rich and happy with you? I want to say, "Hey, let's plan a trip to Paris!" and have my friends say, "Great! When shall we go? Where do you want to stay?" instead of "Oh, I can't afford it" or "I can't take the time off work."

> **Zillionaires know they have a zillionaire's life and they share their wealth.**

I think tips are tithes. I like to tip well—it's an extra blessing to someone who has provided a service to me and will appreciate a little bit extra. I also like to tithe to business owners. Sometimes I buy something I don't need, just to give a sale to someone who needs to make one. Sometimes I pay more for goods or services than I need to, but I am happy to pay. That is not an invitation to Sharks to take advantage of me, but just an acknowledgment that I appreciate someone who knows their own value and charges me accordingly. Not many financial advisors will give you advice to pay top dollar, but if I like the product or service, I am happy to pay extra for quality.

Blessings in, blessings out. That is joy. That is happiness. That is the Zillionaire mindset: making money, having fun, doing good, and sharing the goodies.

Enlightenment Is More Fun Than Resentment

The Jewish Talmud states: "A person will be called upon to account, on Judgment Day, for all permitted pleasures he might have enjoyed but did not." Don't you just love the idea that you will have to answer for it if you don't enjoy your life? Can you picture God asking, like a father reprimanding his daughter, "Did you have all the fun you could have had today, young lady?"

The truth is simple: life is rich and wonderful, and the more we appreciate it, the happier we become.

The Buddhists say that before enlightenment you chop wood and carry water, and after enlightenment you chop wood and carry water. In the Sufi stories, I noticed that often after a disciple became enlightened, he became a merchant. He would sell goods, provide value, receive value, and live simply. The truth is simple: life is rich and wonderful, and the more we appreciate it, the happier we become. You have to be happy now—you can't wait until your goals are achieved. The moment of achievement only lasts a moment. Then there's always another goal, another game to win, another vacation to take, another dollar to earn. Revel in the daily wins, the little joys, and you will be happy every day.

Time magazine, in an article on happiness, stated that often happiness is based on comparison to others. If you have a three-bedroom house and your neighbors have two-bedroom houses, you're happy. But if you have a three-bedroom house and everyone around you has four bedrooms, you're dissatisfied. That's only the viewpoint from the neighborhood, though, not the viewpoint from the stars. On the Zillionaire Scale, there will always be people who have more bedrooms and those who have fewer bedrooms. And there will be people with no bedrooms at all. Which end of the scale are you going to focus your attention on? Are you going to look down the scale and feel rich like a Zillionaire, or up the scale and feel poor like a Zero? Are you going to look up the scale and be a bitter and envi-ous Angry Tuna? Or look down the scale, feel guilty and burn your own bedroom down because someone else doesn't have one, like a Timid Tuna victim? Comparisons can inspire you to do better, or defeat you, depending on how you view it.

I heard a story about two farmers who lived next to each other. One farmer had a beautiful cow, and the other farmer didn't have a cow.

One day, God appeared to the farmer without a cow and said, "I will grant you one wish. Today, you can have anything you desire. What do you want?"

The farmer said, "Kill my neighbor's cow."

Isn't that sad? He didn't wish for a better cow, or two cows, or a herd of cows. His wish was for his neighbor to be brought low. He wanted equality with his neighbor, but equality in his limited view meant they both were poorer instead of both being richer. That's Angry Tuna thinking. A Shark might say, "Kill my neigh-bor's cow and give me ten cows." But he's creating another Angry Shark on the other side of the fence who's going to want to retali-ate. So now both farmers spend all their time, energy, and money on war machinery to kill each other's cows. It's Zero thinking in a zero-sum game. Zillionaire farmers would get together and find a way to build a herd of cows—enough for each of them, with a sur-plus to share.

Paranoia is the fear that the world is out to get you. Pronoia is the faith that the world is out to help you. There are two kinds of people in life: The people who say "Yum!" and the people who say "Yuck!" Let all of us pronoiacs band together and hum "Yum!"

In a Zillionaire World Everyone's Win Is Your Win

At each meeting of WRS, one of my networking groups, we share with the others at our table about a topic of the day. Whenever the topic is "Tell about your greatest business success," I have noted with interest that people rarely focus on the award they won or the big contract they got. They don't talk about the fame, acknowledgment, raises, promotions, or prizes they won. They talk about what they helped *others* win. One after the other, with glowing smiles, each person mentions a particular client that they helped to solve a problem or gain a cherished desire. Their faces shine as they tell their favorite story of the client they helped to win a $7 million contract, or the client they helped overcome their fear of public speaking who got a standing ovation. Joyful energy permeates the room. People who can revel in other people's happiness are the biggest winners in life. They're winning vicariously all the time—it's a constant adrenaline happiness rush.

That is the gift that keeps giving to you: when you help others, their win is your win.

That is the gift that keeps giving to you: when you help others, their win is your win. Their success is your success; their happiness your happiness. When someone in my workshop walks into class excited over the good fortune that they just can't believe happened to them, their excitement and joy spills over to me, and it is mine as completely as it is theirs. When I attended the Worthwhile Referral Sources Annual Awards banquet one year, I clapped loudly for all of my friends who won. When one gentleman came up to me afterwards and said, "Sorry you didn't win anything this year, Chellie," I looked at him in astonishment.

"Four out of five of the top winners thanked me from the podium and said I helped them get where they were. I think I'm the biggest winner in the room!"

To know this joy is why teachers teach, and why parents are proud of their children. Because giving an assist is just as valuable as scoring points in the game themselves. Touchdowns are made by teams, not individuals. The quarterback throws the ball, but he has to have a receiver. If you are on a team, you are already a winner.

Neil Armstrong walked on the moon. Just as a fellow human being, I participated in his adventure; I stood outside my house where I could see the TV and the moon in the sky at the same time. I watched him take that "one small step for a man, one giant leap for mankind." Yes, yes, me too, Neil! I'm there with you! My taxes helped build your ship. Your win is my win. Send out spaceships.

So look forty houses down to the right and forty houses down to the left, and be of service. Maybe forty still seems like a lot. How about eleven?

Take time to savor your achievements, and celebrate those of the others around you. Bask in the glory, then relax and enjoy the day. Warm in the sunshine, chart the path of raindrops, learn from a book, channel surf the TV, listen to a teacher, marvel at a painting, ponder a philosophy, enjoy a movie, a comedian, or a play. Have dinner with a friend, join a sports team, indulge in a hobby. Walk on the beach. Invite someone else to walk on the beach with you. Feel blessed. Feel rich. Every day you do this is living a rich life.

So look forty houses down to the right and forty houses down to the left, and be of service. Maybe forty still seems like a lot. How about eleven? We remember the horrors of fanaticism when the World Trade Center was blown to bits on 9/11, but perhaps it is time to give new meaning to the number eleven. How about this: Make eleven people happy today, tell eleven people you love them, give eleven dollars to charity, praise eleven firefighters, smile at eleven police, help eleven people, eat eleven licorice jelly beans. Remember the 11th Commandment, wear eleven Mardi Gras beads, put eleven gold coins in your pocket, say eleven prayers at eleven o'clock. Commemorate 9/11 with positive elevens, instead of more anger, retribution, and sorrow. Let some good come out of those thousands of deaths, instead of more thousands of deaths.

Sow joy and love and money, Zi-11-ionaire, and so shall you reap.

Let us enjoy life and help others do the same. What we think is what we create. Think better thoughts and more Dolphins will swim into your life. Send out ships to bring home the treasures you seek. Count your money and manage your storehouse. Count your blessings, and value the time of your life. Keep your eye on the lighthouse during the storms, and it will guide you to the harbors of happiness. Choose beliefs that make you happy, and let others do likewise in peace.

> **Karma is the law of cause and effect. You are the cause. The effects are the ones you created.**

Karma is the law of cause and effect. You are the cause. The effects are the ones you created. Grace is the gift that allows you to change and the knowledge that enriches your experience of life. When you learn how to fish, you'll have more abundance in your life. Then teach fishing. When we inculcate the Zillionaire strategies, we will have wealth in our work, harmony in our home, and serenity in our spirit. But like the witches' brew—eye of newt, toe of frog, wing of bat, hair of dog—we have to put *all* the ingredients in the cauldron. If we leave anything out, we get a different result, and what we intended as Love Potion #9 comes out as Pickle Juice #10 instead.

Oh, some Angry Tuna will probably spread the gossip that using that analogy is proof that I'm a witch and deal in black magic. Right. Me and J.K. Rowling and Harry Potter. Call 1-800-GET-A-GRIP.

Laugh. Lighten up. Open your Clown Chakra.

Fishing class is now over. Turn off the lights on your way out. I'm shutting down my computer and putting the sign on the door.

Gone fishing.

About the Author

photo by Starla Fortunato

After a first career in musical theater, Chellie Campbell owned a business management firm with thirteen employees for twelve years. In 1990, she combined her gift for public speaking with her financial expertise to develop an eight-week workshop designed to treat money disorders—spending bulimia and income anorexia. Chellie is the author of *The Wealthy Spirit: Daily Affirmations for Financial Stress Reduction*, which was a book of the week on the Laura Schlessinger radio show and a GlobalNet book-of-the-month selection. She has been quoted in *Good Housekeeping*, *Lifetime*, *Essence*, *Woman's World*, and more than fifteen popular books. She created and teaches the Financial Stress Reduction workshops in the Los Angeles area and gives programs throughout the country.

Chellie holds a B.A. from the University of California at Santa Barbara, is Past President of the Los Angeles Chapter of the National Association of Women Business Owners, and was the 1994 Los Angeles District Small Business Administration Women in Business Advocate. An avid poker player, she plays No-Limit Texas Hold'em tournaments in Los Angeles and Las Vegas, and enjoys birding, science fiction, and chocolate. She lives with her roommate, Shelley, and one fat cat, Mr. Kitty, in Los Angeles. For more information, visit her website at www.chellie.com.

NOTES

NOTES

NOTES